LADY PREACHER

LADY PREACHER

BRENDA CARRADINE

TATE PUBLISHING
AND ENTERPRISES, LLC

Published by Tate Publishing & Enterprises, LLC
127 E. Trade Center Terrace | Mustang, Oklahoma 73064 USA
1.888.361.9473 | www.tatepublishing.com

Tate Publishing is committed to excellence in the publishing industry. The company reflects the philosophy established by the founders, based on Psalm 68:11,
"The Lord gave the word and great was the company of those who published it."

Book design copyright © 2013 by Tate Publishing, LLC. All rights reserved.
Cover design by Rtor Maghuyop
Interior design by Jomel Pepito

Published in the United States of America
ISBN: 978-1-61862-645-5
1. Religion / Christian Ministry / Preaching
2. Religion / Christian Life / Women's Issues
13.02.25

Dedication

*T*his book is dedicated to all the lady preachers, great and small. In this generation of fear and despondency, you, the lady preacher, have risen to the challenge by refusing to be defeated by the winds of controversy and indecisiveness. From every nation throughout the world, God's women have extended their arms of mercy to the faint and lonely at heart. You are a salutary warrior, and your unwavering, unshakeable stance is likened to a pillar in Zion—strong and erect, firm and ever resilient.

May this book enlighten, encourage, and inspire you to continue in the fight for peace as you, the lady preacher, proudly confront the many ills of our society simply for no other reason than to proclaim the acceptable year of the Lord's favor.

Acknowledgements

To God be the glory for the great things he has done!

Special thanks to my loving husband, friend, and pastor, Bishop Ernest E. Carradine Sr.

To my children: Jonathan, Megan, Keisha, Whitney, and Ernest Jr. I love you dearly!

In memory of my loving father, Hillie Williams Jr. Daddy, you taught me how to stand up for righteousness. I promise you I will always do that!

Cordlise Udeoma and LaDonna Vick, thank you both for encouraging me to pursue this project. I owe it all to you.

To my inner circle, the "cot bearers of International Harvest Christian Fellowship Church," I appreciate your unconditional love and support. It has truly been immeasurable.

And last, but certainly not least, to my precious mother, Elizabeth. I miss you so much; you will forever be a delightsome land.

Table of Contents

Introduction

*P*erhaps you are wondering how this book, *Lady Preacher*, came to be. Well, I conducted my first women's conference over fifteen years ago at a private Bible chalet on the tranquil mountains of Okutama, Japan. We met in a small, cozy flat for the question-and-answer session I entitled "Women Called to Ministry."

As I stood in the far corner of the room, I watched as the ladies scurried in, each one pressing to find a comfortable seat. Like girl scouts encircled around a campfire, they sat around the room with their legs crossed and their arms folded, attentively watching as Prophetess Cynthia Steele repositioned her chair and started the meeting. Shortly after the opening prayer, the women anxiously began to open up, pitching questions at her faster than she was able to answer them. As for me, I could only shake my head and say with immense satisfaction and glee, "Father, thank you for telling me to do this. This is really good!"

No sooner than the session ended, the women began to joyfully express their dreams and enthusiasm. In fact, many of them told me the only reason they attended the conference in the first place was they heard there was going to be an opportunity for them to ask questions about their ministerial call. They had some pressing concerns, many of which their pastors and leaders had probably avoided or perhaps reluctantly elected to discuss. By and large, their inquiries were not going to be satisfied or appeased by generalized disclosure. These ladies wanted specific answers to specific questions. For instance, their most pressing inquisition was "Why do some of the leaders in the presbytery exclude women from the oratory platform of ministry when the Bible clearly pronounces their momentous contributions?" To emphasize their point, they proudly showcased the ministry gifts of faithful female icons such as Deborah, Esther, Huldah, and Anna.

For a moment, I felt somewhat melancholy as the ladies voiced their feelings of rejection, apprehension, anger, and uncertainty. I regret that I was forced to admit that I was no stranger to their feelings of despair. I knew all too well why they felt the way they did. "Why would God give me the unction to preach," they asked, "then tell me I'm not allowed to do so?" "If I truly belong in this sacred place, I need to know how to recognize God's voice, walk in the anointing, and preach with power and conviction. I also need to know how I'm expected to act and behave." "What do I do if I'm hurt or offended by others' disapproval of me or my ministry?" and, "Am I justified in leaving a church that blatantly rejects my calling?"

Thank God! As the meeting progressed, the despondency began to subside. The more the ladies shared, the more I was beginning to sense a subtle rise of empowerment and confidence. Soon humility, gratitude, and anxiety collided. To my delight, the ladies' defensive stance was weaning.

Through the words of the lady preacher, the atmosphere miraculously changed. The women were boldly and fearlessly challenged to not only reassess their own ideas and beliefs concerning the generalities of church ministry, but to rediscover God's plan for their own personal lives and ministry. The prophetess pointedly stated, "It doesn't matter what anyone else thinks about your call to ministry. What matters is how you feel about it and why. Do you even believe you belong here? And what have you been called to do? Why did God choose you?"

Her questions no doubt brought the ladies another step closer toward understanding their divine purpose. It was obvious by the meeting's end that the ladies were candidly relieved. "Okay," they said, "maybe there really is a place in ministry for me." Although their faces revealed a hint of perplexity, through it all, they knew God had truly called them to do something great. Still, some didn't know what that something was, but they knew in time they'd find out. Jovially I smiled as God spoke to me once again.

It was at that precise moment, in lieu of all I had witnessed throughout the meeting, that I was inspired to write a book and call it *Lady Preacher*. "Lord," I said, "you're taking me down an unmarked path. I don't know if I'm ready to go, but I'm willing." Today I can honestly say writing this book has been a spiritually transforming experience. At times I felt inadequate, other times triumphant and heroic, but never dismal or defeated.

Lady Preacher is a guideline that will instruct, inform, and encourage you to pursue your purpose and call to ministry. It is not a how-to book. It is a because-of book. Yes, because you have acknowledged a calling to preach the gospel of Jesus Christ, this book was designed to equip you for service. Consider this book a starter kit to ministry.

Although *Lady Preacher* was especially created with women preachers in mind, anyone in any area of ministry can benefit from it. The information discussed in this book is amiable and gratifying. It is a mature guideline that addresses the issues that affect Christians everywhere. Whether you are a man or woman, this book will greatly enhance your understanding of ministry in today's world.

Everywhere I go, women ask me, "What do I do with the passion God has placed within me?" No doubt this book will help you to answer that question and perhaps many, many, more.

In spite of the discrimination (still existent in ministry today), many women are finding their place in ministry. They are no longer hiding their talents in the earth, suppressing their call to greatness, nor conforming to the impressions of a differentiating society. No, they're getting in the book and discovering what God has to say about their lives and the roles they play in today's ministry.

Each chapter of this book addresses ministry from a completely different perspective. The first five chapters deal with the preliminary instructions of ministry. These chapters are foundational and are filled with practical information. They also answer the age-old question, "Are women supposed to preach?" and the truth behind head coverings.

The next five chapters confront the ills of ministry. Unfortunately ministry has an ugly side, yet I will address these problems with tact and sensitivity as I prepare you for what I've labeled "ministry's reality."

The final three chapters will release you to discover the woman in you. You will be inspired as we discuss such issues as self-reflection, meditation, sisters loving and caring for sisters, and the art of succession.

Lady preacher, may you be just as inspired to read this book as I was in writing it! Enjoy it, recommend it, and share it with a friend!

Men and Women Together in Ministry

> When God created man, he made him in the likeness (image) of God. He created them male and female and blessed them. And when they were created, he called them "man"
>
> Genesis 5:1-2 (NIV)

What was in the heart of God when he created mankind? Did he create male and female as equals with similar aspirations, intelligence, and identity? Do their distinctive roles, personalities, and characteristics enable them to fulfill God's plan on the earth today? To answer these questions, we'll begin by disclosing the fundamental truths impeding male and female cooperation. Why is there so much tension among the sexes? And who is to blame for their disharmony? Well, let's start by examining the rise and fall of the first family, God's prototype, Adam and Eve.

Like many of you, my first encounter with male and female began in the home. Fortunately, I grew up with both of my parents, and I knew all too well the difference between male and female. It didn't take very long for me to discover which parent was soft and sympathetic and which was strong and assertive. When male and female flow together in concert, they exemplify God's structural blueprint for the family and his ideal design for cohabitation and the continuation of life.

In coinciding with the scriptures, we perceive that the concept of oneness was clearly defined in the mind of God. God created man as a reflection of himself. He created him complete with the distinct ability to think, act, articulate, and celebrate life. Adam, whose name in Hebrew means "man, human being, or mankind," (1) was created with the woman within himself. While Adam lay in a deep sleep, God reached inside of him, took out a rib, and created for him a suitable companion.

Eve was the compliment and completion of man. She was created in the image of God with all of the fundamental qualities Adam possessed. Genesis 2:22 says that God presented Eve to Adam as a bride to a groom—not as a token or a trophy, but as a gift. She was to Adam an intrepid supporter and helper, but more importantly, she was a faithful, impassioned partner.

Although the two of them were similar in numerous ways, they were very different. And it was those differences that caused them to fit so perfectly together. This is the whole genesis of man, that male and female represent God's image through their union. God, with fervent compassion, not only created us for himself but for one another.

We were designed and created to enjoy the pleasures of fellowship and friendship—together. By and large, God created us to complement one another in both design and existence. We were not meant to function independently of the other. Even the continuation of life is dependent on male and female cooperation.

The Fall and Role Differentiation

> To the woman he said, "I will greatly increase your pains in childbearing; with pain you will give birth to children. Your desire will be for your husband and he will rule over you."
>
> Genesis 3:16 (NIV)

As a result of Adam and Eve's admission to sin, male and female relationships became grossly distorted. Sue and Larry Richards, authors of *Every Woman in the Bible*, make this comment concerning the fall: "after the fall and the consequences of sin were pronounced, women's affections were then directed from pleasing God to pleasing men" (8). As a result, women everywhere were forced to equalitarianism and female subjugation. The Richards explain their theory further by stating, "Husband in this text is interpreted *ish*, Hebrew for the word 'man' or 'mankind'; thus suggesting that women post fall would not only desire to please or seek approval from their own husbands, but men or mankind in general" (8). This is a very important thought when we consider the condition of women down through the years.

This historical event actually marks the turning point in the genesis of female separation and egotism. Again, I must reiterate the fact that this convergence was never in the heart of God. To him, women have always been equal in value and importance. And still, many centuries later, he grieves as his daughters struggle with feelings of inferiority as a result of male domination and chauvinism.

Undoubtedly, Satan had a plan. He knew if he could keep male and female apart, he could not only prevent us from producing human seed and natural life, but godly seed and spiritual life as well. You question how it is possible for Satan to so easily separate us when we were created to be together. Well, it's actually quite simple; he puts us one against the other by creating surges of power and supremacy between us. These surges of power I've called "power wedges." And they slowly but surely disintegrate the fabric of a relationship. When you look at the intrinsic composition of a power wedge, you'll find it is in and of itself a demonic vice designed to not only divide and conquer but to rank and stratify superiority. A power wedge will show up unannounced everywhere and in everything. Whether a couple is trying to handle the bills, do laundry, or discipline the children, the setting is practically irrelevant. Power wedges simply emerge when communication and interaction is void of mutual submission, respect, and kindness.

Alongside authority, God gave male and female the desire to rule and dominate. However, we both have to learn how to operate in that power with respect for one another. Male and female relationships will never flow respectfully without submission and order. Submission and order must operate simultaneously, paralleling one another in power and productivity.

Perhaps if male and female roles were more clearly defined, fewer power wedges would emerge. Coincidentally, if male and female do not understand their specific roles, power struggles will ultimately surface, and the bonding process will be intermittently disturbed by the need to take over and/or take charge. Years ago, Myles Monroe coined a phrase still popular in our Christian sects. He said, "If you don't know the purpose of a thing, you will abuse it." *Selah.*

In addition, general statistics ardently contend that over fifty percent of marriages today, whether in or out of the church, will end in divorce. I believe many, if not most, of these marriages dissolve as a result of issues relating to role confusion, role reversal, and superiority complexes.

I personally understand the destructive nature of a power wedge. In the early years of my marriage, my husband and I completely lacked the necessary tools for building a solid relationship. As a result, our marriage suffered greatly.

My role as a wife and helper was difficult for me to accept. This, however, was primarily because of what I'd seen and experienced growing up. In my mind, everything my husband said to me I interpreted as a threat or a means of controlling me, and frankly speaking, I resented it. To make matters worse, he was none the wiser, unwittingly using his power and position to further escalate the hostility already growing between us.

Since neither one of us fully understood our responsibilities in the relationship, we were constantly competing for power. Bottom line, he wanted to be respected and appreciated as the head of the home, and I wanted to be the boss. Surprisingly enough, what we really wanted was to cease fire and live together in peace, each one doing their part to maximize and capitalize on our cumulative assets.

Around 1991 or 1992, some friends rescued us by inviting us to attend a marriage seminar with Apostle Louis Greenup Jr., a.k.a. "The Marriage Doctor." The principles and concepts we learned at that seminar were simple and elementary, yet they totally changed the course of our marriage. Finally, after many years of struggling, the light bulb came on, and for the first time we were experiencing harmony and cooperation in our relationship. For me, this was the beginning of my understanding of the helper role.

Created to Be a Helper

> The Lord God said, "It is not good for man to
> be alone. I will make a helper suitable for him."
>
> Genesis 2:18 (NIV)

When you understand who you are and who you were created to be, there is no remorse or shame. You can do what you have been called to do and do it with excellence, precision, and confidence. For many women today, the idea of women as helpers is demeaning and degrading. Undoubtedly, since many of the Old Testament encounters posed ill-willed offenses against women (polygamy and penal injustice), women liberators found overwhelming evidence to support this unfortunate view. But all in all this idea supports an inaccurate depiction of God's initial purpose for creating womankind. I agree the fall in and of itself was devastating to the livelihood of women. However, it had no permanent effect on the destiny of Christian women today. God's purpose for women is ensured by the promise in the new covenant. Jesus nailed the former infraction to his cross, preserving God's original promise for all mankind. That is why Jesus was called the second Adam. Christ gave us a new beginning. In fact, through him, the penalty and consequences of the fall were completely reversed, and women were exonerated and restored to their rightful place beside the men (Adam).

In referring to the complexity of the role of helper, *supporter* is by far the grandest definition. *Support* means "to bear with, to take sides with, or to hold up and serve." *Ezer* in the Hebrew means "helper—to help, support, or assist." As a woman, I can serve as a helper and not feel inferior because God himself was a helper. See Psalms 30:2,10; 33:20; and 121:1. The Greek word for the Holy Spirit is *parakletos*. *Paraklete* means "one called alongside to help."

Women were created to lend support by helping the brethren maintain readiness. God showed me this one evening as my husband and I were sitting together watching a movie. In this drama, the boss of this corporation kept calling his assistant the "wingman." I asked my husband, who happened to be an Air Force Chief at the time, "What is a wing man?"

He said, "The wing man is a point man (in this particular case a pilot) who warns the lead man of incoming dangers from directions only he at his vantage point can see."

"Wow," I said. "I think I like that." I would venture to say I'm more than a suitable helper, supporter, and assistant. I, too, am a capable wingman. God gifted women everywhere with sensitivity and wisdom, thus enabling us with the skills and ability to successfully model the helper role in the male-female relationship.

Disadvantages of Being a Helper: Submitting One to the Other

*I*n order for male and female oneness to work effectively, we both have to feel needed and appreciated by the other—respected, able to openly share and converse with one another without intimidation or fear.

Consequently, I realize how frustrating it is trying to help someone who doesn't want to be helped. Whether it is in the home, on the job, or in the church, submitting to people who dishonor you as a helper is extremely difficult. The Bible tells us to "submit to one another out of reverence for Christ" (Ephesians 5:21, NIV). This scripture alone could serve as a cure all for male and female disharmony. Paul taught and apparently believed in the principles of divine order; the male serving and leading as the head, and the female serving and leading as a helper.

Thus, he supported equality and encouraged men and women to love, support, and submit to one another in respect to Christ and the overall plan of God for mankind. This request was not only for the advancement of God's kingdom, but for peace among the brethren as well.

Women as Helpers in Ministry

Women have always played a viable role in the scriptures. From Genesis to Revelation, we have served as helpers supporting, and at times, even leading under the auspices of the Holy Spirit. Deborah, for instance, was a judge and a prophetess, who, at the Lord's command, instructed the Israelites to battle against Sisera, the military commander of the army of King Jabin of Hazor. Deborah's significance to women in ministry is highlighted in Judges 4:4 as she is presented as "Deborah, a prophetess, the wife of Lappidoth, was judging Israel at the time."

In this story, Deborah summoned Barak to lead the Israelites against the king. Surprisingly, in lieu of Barak's confidence in Deborah's leadership, he refused to go to war if she would not accompany him. In the end, the victory was credited to Deborah the lady preacher instead of Barak and the men of war.

Then there was Esther, the queen of Ahasuerus, who saved her people from genocide. Also, there was Ruth, the favored Moabite, wife of Boaz and a great ancestor of Christ. Both of these women have books in the Bible commemorating their momentous contributions—not only to religion and theology, but to literature and the arts as well.

In spite of the patriarchal limitations of that time, God still used women mightily to alter and shape the course of biblical history. God's original plan for male and female was not impeded by Satan's deceptive plot. In fact, as one generation recedes and gives way to another, God always has a remnant of people, both male and female, who will serve him together in the fields of ministry.

—

Are Women Supposed to Preach?

*F*or some of you, preaching is fairly new. Though this book does not cover many of the expository concepts of preaching, it is helpful to know how to exegete the scriptures more efficiently. You may find this information handy as we prepare to study this chapter.

Years ago, I learned three important concepts that enabled me to better understand and interpret the scriptures. They were as follows:

1. Observation: You should always observe the content in its completed text. What's actually going on? Who are the characters involved? And where does the story take place? What actually happened (the surrounding circumstances) before and after the text in question?

2. Interpretation: You need to interpret (analyze) the author's original intent (idea or mindset) for writing the text. You can do this by asking

yourself, "What did the author mean when he or she said what they said?" "Why did he or she say that?" and "what was the author trying to convey?"

3. Application: You should incorporate the understanding of the scripture with practical application. "How can I apply what I now know and understand to my daily life?" and "how can I accurately relay that knowledge to others?"

Should Women Preach?

Before we go any farther, it is imperative that you, the lady preacher, settle this question in your heart. Is a women supposed to preach? If you don't settle this issue now, you will never be able to accept and embrace your call to ministry.

Formally, women who preached in both the Old and New Testaments were called "prophetesses." Prophet means "one who utters or speaks the divine revelation of God." The Bible directly identifies at least seven women in scripture who ministered in the office of a prophetess: Miriam, Moses's sister (Exodus 15:20); Deborah (Judges 4:4); Isaiah's wife (Isaiah 8:3); Huldah (2 Chronicles 34:22); Anna (Luke 2:36-38); and Phillip's four daughters (Acts 21:9).

In lieu of the evidence presented, there is no doubt God approved the use of women in ministry, both preaching and teaching the inspired word. However, when we examine the following scriptures, it would appear that women (perhaps these women in particular) were prohibited from pulpit ministry and speaking in the local assembly. Ironically, Paul, a leader who fervently supported spiritual freedom and equality, was singularly responsible for executing this conflicting mandate. Why would Paul do that? There had to be a logical explanation.

Dispersing the Confusion

> And every woman who prays or prophesies [preaches, speaks forth, or declares] with her head uncovered dishonors her head—it is just as though her head were shaved.
>
> 1 Corinthians 11:5 (NIV)

> For man did not come from woman, but woman from man; neither was man created for woman, but for man. For this reason and because of the angels, the woman ought to have a sign of authority on her head. In the Lord, however, woman is not independent of man nor is man independent of woman. For as woman came from man, man so also is born of woman. But everything comes from God.
>
> 1 Corinthians 11: 8-12 (NIV)

> For God is not a God of disorder but of peace. As in all the congregations of the saints. Women should remain silent in the churches. They

are not to speak, but must be in submission
as the law says. If they want to inquire about
something, they should ask their own husbands
at home, for it is disgraceful for a woman to
speak in church.

Corinthians 14:33-35 (NIV)

A woman should learn in quietness and full
submission. I do not permit a woman to teach
or to have authority over a man; she must be
silent. For Adam was formed first, then Eve.
And Adam was not the one deceived; it was the
woman who was deceived and became a sinner.

1 Timothy 2:11-12 (NIV)

At first glance, it would seem the plight for women
in ministry was rather hopeless. But let's reexamine a
few important points. Now, it is a given fact that God
used women in ministry. However, prior to the death
and resurrection of Jesus Christ, women were bound by
the laws of society. Every social system, including the
patriarchal religious institutions of that day, vehemently
supported male subjugation.

During that time, women were completely
reliant upon the mercy of men, not only for life's
everyday existence, but for their spiritual growth and
development as well. Life for women changed only as a
result of Calvary, nothing else. In fact, when Jesus died
on the cross, he gave us our spiritual rights back, and
not only our spiritual rights, but our legal and moral,
rights as well.

Before Calvary, women were strictly prohibited from freely participating in the worship service. As was the custom of that day, the women sat in the back of the synagogue behind the men where their hearing and visibility was terribly obscured. You can only imagine the problems this arrangement created. For one, the good news of the gospel was being preached and demonstrated, and the women were elated and anxious to participate. And, of course, who could argue their aspirations? Their affections were completely understandable. Surely everyone in that day, whether they were a believer or not, wanted to see and hear (firsthand, if possible) the miracles Jesus performed through the acts of the apostles and to be an eyewitness to the development of the New Testament church. This is a true fact concerning these women, who for centuries were bound by the law and now by the blood of Jesus Christ they would be free to express their God-given rights and privileges.

Christ reorganized the institution of worship by tearing down the walls of separatism and enveloping and inviting women of all nationalities to serve and participate in the worship experience; that's what the new church ultimately unveiled—cohesion and collaboration among the sexes.

Women in the Church

Paul knew women everywhere had been emancipated. It was no more "business as usual." However, he also knew without order and instruction the potential problems their liberation could, and eventually did, present in the New Testament churches.

In the commentary notes of the Life Application Bible, theologians and Bible scholars suggests that Paul literally silenced the women (temporarily, not permanently) in the churches at Ephesus and Corinth because they were causing insurmountable confusion. Incidentally, when you study the culture and climate of these two churches, this interpretation is most fitting.

The churches were newly established and lacking order. In fact, Paul had to frequently address problems within these two churches, especially Corinth. The church, for example, was fighting over spiritual gifts and leaders, abusing spiritual privileges, and disrespecting the sacraments, not to mention practicing immorality and heresy. Thus, the situation with the newly liberated women was nothing more than an addendum to the many problems already facing this fast-growing and fluently gifted church. Apparently, these women were outspoken, unlearned in the scriptures, and zealous to share their spiritual gifts, testimonies, and expressions. But as a result of doing so, they caused a terrible uproar in the church.

Perhaps the women began to rebel against the traditional customs by refusing to wear their head coverings, intermingling with the men during the worship services, or, worst of all, protesting disapproval for the former religious practices and the clergy. At any rate, their behavior was unacceptable and, honestly speaking, revolutionary. Bottom line, the men were simply not accustomed to their behavior. No respectable Jewess would publically challenge a man in public. Yet these women apparently did.

In all reality, zeal may have been the reason for the ladies' misconduct. Nevertheless, they dishonored the Lord by aggressively and publicly challenging the men. Paul wanted women to understand that being free in Christ did not mean disrespecting male leadership. In fact, divine order is never obsolete. I believe Paul handled the situation appropriately, no differently than it should be handled in our churches today. Through Christ, women have been given the opportunity to not only share the gospel message but to grow and excel in other sects of society as well (business, medicine, politics, technology, and so forth). But, as it relates to the church, males and females must submit to one another in love if Christian freedoms and liberties are to be expressed without limitations and boundaries.

Head Coverings

As we examine the issue of head coverings, we must first take the time to completely analyze the text recorded in 1 Corinthians 11:1-16. Please get your Bibles so you can follow along. It will help you understand what Paul was thinking about when he spoke these words to the Corinthian church. Again, theologians have conflicting arguments concerning head coverings. However, because it is an important issue for some in the church today, I will address it. Moreover, Paul raises some very interesting points as he converses with us in scripture. Let's look at what Paul has to say:

Verse 1: Paul starts out by commending the church for their faith in his wisdom and "holding to the traditions." What traditions? Obedience to God's divine order and the wearing of head (cloth) coverings. This was, after all, a sign of respect for male headship.

Verse 3: Paul confirms the order of submission and recognizes the source from which one exists (God is the head of Christ, Christ is the head of the church, and man is the head of woman). This verse is not suggesting superiority stratification. Quite commonly, no one would suggest that Jesus is inferior to God. Just the same, no one should suggest that women are inferior to men. The Bible says of the Godhead the two are one. Yet Jesus willingly submitted to His father's authority, just as women should willingly submit to their husband's authority.

Verses 5-6: Paul says a woman should have her head covered. Covered with what? Let's reiterate the customs of the times. Women wore tunics or head wraps as a sign of respect and honor for themselves and male headship. During those days, it was disrespectful for a woman to cut or shave her head. In fact, women wore their hair very long, as they were not to resemble or appear to oppose or disrespect men

Verse 7: Paul not only discusses female coverings but male coverings as well. Men did not wear head coverings (even today, if a man wears a hat inside, it's considered disrespectful).

Verse 14: Paul says even nature inherently agrees with this theology by suggesting that men should not wear their hair long as to resemble a woman. Paul wanted to ensure gender differentiation. It was important that male and female roles were clearly defined, and Paul didn't want the women's newfound liberties to be misinterpreted, causing confusion in the church. In other words, though women were given the right to express themselves spiritually, they were still expected to act and behave like women.

Verses 8-10: Paul reminds us of the importance of recognizing God's order (he says, "Even the angels understand divine order"). Again, he says in Verse 10, her covering, headpiece, and/or hair is a sign of her submission and respect to authority.

Verses 11-12: Paul showcases the original plan of God by recalling male and female inter-dependency. "In the Lord," he says, "we operate together and co-exist as one within the body of Christ. Together we are complete."

Verses 13-14: Paul seems to offer debate in these verses by saying, "You be the judged in this matter." What matter? The appropriate sign of authority for a woman when she preaches (prophesizes) or prays in the church. He compares this question to how the order of things appear in nature. (Again, men didn't wear long hair to avoid resembling a woman).

Verses 15-16: Paul concludes this discussion by saying, "Her hair has been given to her as a covering" (the woman's hair represents respect for male headship). He finalizes this issue as he continues, "If anyone wants to be contentious about this, we have no other practice, nor do the other churches." In other words, Paul is saying you decide what is best for your congregation; just endeavor to maintain order and respect for the house of God (NIV).

What do you think the previous scriptures are actually saying? Does the text suggest women shouldn't preach? Or, if they do, whether or not they need male covering? According to what we have learned in the scriptures, women are permitted to preach, and they can do so without male authorization. God's use of woman in the scriptures confirms this. Nevertheless, in reference to divine order and women presenting themselves respectfully and appropriately in the house of God, Paul has made his stand very clear. However, he left the issue of head coverings to the decision-making bodies of the church.

Our final argument is found in the first epistle of Timothy 2:12: "Adam was not the one that was deceived and became a sinner." Paul seems to suggest that women are perhaps more vulnerable to deception than men; possibly requiring a male covering, protection, and support.

When examining the intrinsic characteristics of women, Paul's statement is understandable. Whereas, women obviously share the more delicate characteristics of creation, both male and female are subject to the wiles of demonic entrapment and deception.

Although women may not necessarily need male authorization to preach, I would venture to say that male support and covering is highly recommended. All in all, it secures safety and offers support. If you notice in Scripture, women are always referred to as "the wife of" or "the daughter of," possibly signifying her support system and/or a sign of male protection.

Review Precepts

1. God created male and female in his own image.

2. The passion to conquer, subdue, and have dominion is a God-given drive mutually shared among human kind, whether male or female.

3. Both male and female are endowed with certain characteristics, qualities, and abilities that only he or she can disclose and perform. Together, they provide completeness as two separately distinct individuals become one.

4. When a man is flowing and operating in his role as the leader (or head), the woman is receptive to her role as a helper and a supporter.

5. God's ideal plan for growth and productivity is identified in the collaborative efforts of mutual submission and agreement.

6. If men and women complement one another (with respect to submission and authority), the will of God can be clearly appreciated, understood, and executed efficiently.

Phenomenal Woman: Selected by God

He said to another man, "Follow me." But the man replied, "Lord, first let me go and bury my father." Jesus said to him, "Let the dead bury their own dead, but you go and proclaim the kingdom of God." Still another said, "I will follow you; but Lord; first let me go back and say good-bye to my family." Jesus replied, "No one who puts his hand to the plow and looks back is fit for service in the kingdom of God.

Luke 9:59-62 (NIV)

Since the tragic events in the garden unfolded, women around the world have felt the impact of discrimination. Despite recent advancements, many patriarchal systems in religion, politics, education, and economics still remain exclusively closed to women. Nevertheless, it's a great day to be a woman! No longer are we suppressing our call to greatness because of stereotypical idioms and societal norms. With the cross before us and Eden behind us, we are progressively moving forward, getting into the book and discovering what God has to say about the roles we play in today's world and ministry. The great emancipator Jesus Christ has set us free from the curse of the law. Henceforth, we are free to express the passions within us, free to challenge ourselves to reach beyond mediocrity, free to be creative and innovate, and free to make an impact on the world around us. *Free!*

Throughout Bible history, women such as Mary Magdalene, Mary Jesus's mother, Phoebe, Tabitha, and Rahab have stood against danger, opposition, and ridicule to trek the roads of passage we now celebrate in ministry today. Respectfully, I'm honored to be named among them. If God can use Mother Theresa to feed and cloth impoverished children in third world nations or Corrie ten Boom to rescue Jewish refugees from Hitler's horrid grip during World War II or perhaps even the eccentric healer and charismatic orator Katherine Kulhman, surely he can use someone like me.

The Call to Ministry

> Anyone who loves father or mother more than me is not worthy of me; anyone who loves son or daughter more than me is not worthy of me, and anyone who does not take his cross and follow me is not worthy of me. Whoever finds his life will lose it, and whoever loses his life for my sake will find it.
>
> Matthew 10:37-39 (NIV)

What does it mean to be called to preach? In 1985, I attended a summer revival in Fort Worth, Texas, where I heard none other than the legendary Rev. Dr. C.A.W. Clark as he spoke these profound words: "If a man can keep from preaching, he ought not to preach." *Selah*!

Preaching is birthed out of a sincere passion to proclaim the gospel message. Every preacher, male or female, who acknowledges this passion must submit their hearts to a metamorphic, life-changing transformation. Perhaps, in theory, your call to ministry may have somehow resembled this ambiguously sketchy description. Yet, in reality, the call in and of itself is difficult to explain and articulate. In a most imminent way, you are moved toward something, but to what, you don't really know. You hear the summons to go, but to where, you're not really sure. Categorically, these riddles avert and perplex you as you stand at the crossroads of indecisiveness and fear. Nevertheless, one thing is certain; God is calling you to greatness, calling you to take up your cross and follow him.

Initially, most of us knew nothing about answering the call of God. Aside from sharing one's own experience with others and hearing others personal testimonies, passion takes sole responsibility for driving you to the climax of acceptance. Had it not, some of you would have found a logical reason for dismissing it altogether. Preachers who join the ranks of ministry out of a sincere passion to preach the gospel do so by faith and faith alone.

Running from the Call

Just the same, the truthful reality remains unchanged; no matter how hard you try to run from the calling, you cannot ignore or refute it—not if it is sure and uncompromising. Like many of you, I too attempted to divert the call by directing my energy elsewhere. I assumed if I took on other positions within the church, God would release me from the call to preach. But, heretofore, nothing can fulfill your passion to preach the gospel if that is what God has called you to do. In fact, you will find no solace in anything else. Your peace is in obeying his will for your life.

Throughout my Christian experience, I have worked in various areas of ministry. Yet the moment God began to push me toward my calling, all of my additional church activities seemed inconsequential. God was agitating me, and I couldn't concentrate on anything above what He was instructing me to do. In contrast, I really did believe He was calling me to ministry. However, a part of me was in serious doubt, and I was simply too afraid to admit it. Amid the disparate uncertainty, I found myself asking those I thought were spiritual, "Do you think God has called me to preach?" Saints, take my advice and don't do that.

At the time, God had not yet confirmed my calling, at least not to me, and that's what I was looking for—manifestation and confirmation. So to some extent, I'm sure I appeared a bit desperate. But in reality, all I wanted was to ensure certainty. I knew the severity and seriousness of accepting the call to preach. (You see, I'd seen the equivalence of a total flop, and I didn't want to consider it haphazardly.)

To make a long story short, I never got "a word from the Lord," at least, not by the admission of man. However, when I finally settled my spirit, God visited me with pointed instructions, telling me exactly what he wanted me to do, who he wanted me to talk to, and where he wanted me to go from there. (For a further study on accepting the call to ministry, refer to Paul's conversion in Acts 9:1-19).

Beloved, God doesn't want you to look to man to interpret the call He has placed in you. God Himself will harvest the seed he has planted in you. In a similar way, God calls us like he called Samuel—by name. And it will do you no good to converse with Eli. Consequently, Eli as a servant of the Most High God has only one responsibility to you, and that is to instruct you to go "lie back down," and if he calls you (again) say, "Speak Lord, for your servant is listening" (1 Samuel 3:8-9, NIV).

No doubt your pastor and leaders are able to discern the ministerial anointing on your life, but they cannot confirm your calling. Only you know if God is actually calling you to preach, and that is a very personal invitation.

Over thirty years ago, about five young men in my hometown church went before the congregation and publicly acknowledged their call to preach. One Sunday, not long after accepting his calling, one of the young men stood up and renounced his decision. Boldly, and I commended him for it, he went before the church and apologized, admitting he'd never been called to preach in the first place. He only did it, he said, because his friends were doing it.

Wrestling with the Call

A novice is as much afraid of his or her public performance as he or she is overzealous and anxious to publicly perform. Nevertheless, new preachers must be tried and tested. Back in the day, years before I accepted my call to ministry, I remember my momma talking about "jack-leg" preachers. Now, for those of you who are not familiar with that term, a jack-leg or boot-leg preacher is slang for an individual who takes advantage of prime-time intermissions in the service to S. A.M. (sneak a message). In short, this is the kind of person you don't ask to pray over the evening meal. He'll start off praying over the chicken, and before long he's prayed for the poor, the sick, the widows, and the church's building fund. In my mind, I can see him stomping his feet and waving a handkerchief in the air as rounded beads of sweat roll down his sunken cheeks, pooling rapidly at the brim of his collar as he feverishly gyrates to the rhythm of his own broken drone. And by the time he actually finishes the painstaking prayer (of course, he closed about three or four times beforehand), the food is cold and the mothers are virulently gathering bowls together for re-warming.

Do you happen to remember any preachers like that? I sure do. Of course, I wasn't quite that bad, but I must admit there were times I did try to get "my preach" on! Fortunately, at the crowning of my ministry, I had a pastor, a chaplain named Rev. Clinton Brantley, who acknowledged my gift and encouraged me to seek the Lord. He told me he saw "fire" in me, and that was enough to prompt me to enquire of the Lord. Like so many of you, I wanted confirmation. However, it was certainly not kosher to solicit it from people. I knew I needed to go to God for spiritual, mental, and emotional grounding, and when I did, that's exactly what He provided. Nevertheless, I wrestled with the call to ministry for the same reasons many of you did. Fear! First and foremost, I feared what others would think of me. After all, I was a woman. Not just a woman, but a woman acknowledging a call to preach the gospel, and in many denominations, that was unheard of.

Traditionally, preaching has been a structurally powered position predominately held by men. And, for the most part, women were not cordially invited. Perhaps if you were raised in religious organizations that did not support or credit women as preachers, you can emphatically understand my mental anguish. I was not only struggling against my own fears and insecurities but against the stigma of what I was taught and raised to believe. I was forced to ask myself the question, "Do I really belong here?"

Beloved, God does not use gender as a prerequisite for dispensing and determining one's spiritual gifts. The Bible says, "You are all sons of God through faith in Christ Jesus, for all of you who were baptized into Christ have clothed yourselves with Christ. There is neither Jew nor Greek, slave or free, male nor female, for you are all one in Christ Jesus. If you belong to Christ, you are Abraham's seed, and heirs according to the promise" (Galatians 3:26-29 NIV).

All and all, I feared failure. I didn't want to fail God nor myself. So for many months I wept, wrestled, and wavered over a decision I was ultimately compelled to make. One evening, as I paced across my dining room floor with tears streaming down my face, I insistently came to the realization that whatever the cost, I couldn't live unless I fulfilled the passion of His calling. I had no other recourse—I had to answer the call.

The Obstacles

I'd venture to say fear is perhaps the primary culprit to answering one's call, but there are many other reasons women are reluctant to respond. In each case, the excuses are usually legitimate, but, frankly speaking, inconsequential. God knows who you are and where you come from, and in His eyes, you are a mighty woman of valor. If you weren't, He would never have called you in the first place.

Whether male or female, I realize the call to serve is solemn, immutable, and sacrificial. Yet history supports the fact that women overall contend with twice as many issues as men. But let's look at a few commonly acknowledged excuses for rebutting the call. Perhaps you can think of a few additional excuses yourself:

- Fear of man
- Fear of failure
- Intimidation
- Pressure to compete
- Feelings of inferiority
- Lack of support
- Fear of rejection
- Timidity
- Ignorance of the word
- Insecurity
- Addicted to vices
- Self hatred
- Personal problems
- Domestic duties
- Lack of formal education

Accepting Your Call

Your first step in ministry is to accept the call. As a matter of fact, your journey begins with that acknowledgment—afterwards, a strict regimen of discipleship, purification, and holiness. Like Samuel, some of you recognized a call to ministry at a very young age. Yet without your help or divine intervention, God has preserved your calling for now, right now. Throughout grade school, college, boyfriends, drugs, etcetera, the devil couldn't kill or steal your divine purpose.

Queen Esther was required to complete twelve months of beautification treatments to prepare herself for King Xerxes's service. And to be considered a candidate for courtship, she had to undergo the rigorous ceremonial washings of oil and myrrh, perfume, aroma therapy, exfoliation, and dieting. Esther was willing to sacrifice her personal desires and possibly even her dignity to fulfill her divine purpose (Esther 2:12-13). Much like Esther, you too have been called "for such a time as this."

At every turn, I see bruised and afflicted people in the mall, on the streets, in the schools, and even in the church. Yet I realize "the spirit of the Lord is upon me, because he hath anointed me to preach the Gospel to the poor; he hath sent me to heal the broken hearted, to preach deliverance to the captives and recovering of sight to the blind, to set at liberty them that are bruised; to preach the acceptable year of the Lord" (Luke 4:18-19, KJV).

This mandate was not given to me alone. God is calling women everywhere to service. If you think about it, what other choice do you have? Where can you hide to divert his presence, his summons? Wherever you go, rest assured he'll find you. Therefore, I admonish you to submit to his purpose and answer the call. God has already called you a phenomenal woman; receive it, accept it, and walk in it, regardless of who refutes it! Whether your calling is poetry reading, writing, prison ministries, advocating human rights for exploited women, drug and alcohol rehabilitation, building shelters for battered women and children, worldwide missions, or intercession, somebody somewhere is waiting for you!

Review Precepts

1. God has always used women to further his agenda on the earth. By and large, women were created to fulfill and complete his divine purpose.

2. Women were never an afterthought in the mind of God. In fact, from the very beginning we were destined to play a significant role in his original plan for mankind.

3. Settle the calling in your own heart. Do not embark upon it if you are ambivalent and indecisive; wait for confirmation.

4. Take full responsibility and pride in your calling.

5. The call to ministry should not be taken lightly. As a matter of fact, you need to know that God is calling you to this sacred posture.

6. To the best of your ability, count up the cost because ministry in and of itself requires total sacrifice.

7. Make sure you understand your calling and your purpose. What did God tell you to do?

Alone with God

*D*aily I am challenged to rectify today what I failed to do yesterday. Much like some of you, I start my day with good intentions. Sometimes, by the grace of God, I manage to get a portion of my assigned tasks accomplished. Other times I miss it altogether. Nevertheless, by day's end, I release myself from the guilt of defeat by admitting it was highly unlikely I was ever going to get it all done in the first place. Though I may have honestly begun my day with high expectations, I fail if I do not adequately consecrate myself before the Lord.

Setting Aside Time for God

Disciplining yourself to commit to a daily regimen of prayer and devotion is essentially the key to ministerial success. Preachers can't afford to let their everyday chores and schedules invade their time alone with God. For woman, this is an especially difficult challenge.

Being alone with God is not only important in building your personal relationship with Christ, but to the advancement of your ministry. As Christians, we have a solemn obligation to the Lord and to ourselves to reserve quality time with him in prayer and devotion. Every day you wake up, you must decide what things are important to accomplish in that day. What is of greatest priority to you? Prayerful time alone with God tops your list.

Just in case you didn't know it, finding time alone with God doesn't just happen; you must make it happen. Of course, that means setting aside a specific time every day where you can meet with the Lord without disruptions or distractions. Now, to acquire that kind of time, you'll need to make some personal sacrifices. You can't sit up late at night, watching television or finalizing the next day's events and think you're going to be alert, and spiritually sensitive come morning. It is totally impossible. Your body will seriously rebel against you. In fact, you'll find yourself falling asleep in between every other verse, losing concentration, and never benefitting from your personal devotion.

Consider how often you've climbed out of bed just in time to get a shower and get to work? Somehow you convince yourself as you're washing your face and humming a few bars of "I Love You Lord" that everything is fine and God is okay with your hurried praise. Though you'd never say it aloud, you're thinking to yourself, *Lord, I did it again. I hope my efforts (my song) will appease you this morning. Perhaps you will give me another chance to get it right… tomorrow. I promise I'll do better tomorrow.* Of course, for some, tomorrow never comes. Nevertheless, you know what God really wants from you, and that is your time and obedience. New believers may get away with that (for a season), but "where much is given, much is expected and required" (Luke 12:48, NIV). When we fail to give God those things he requires, our song becomes a mere formality for our lack of discipline and obedience. God wants the first fruits of our day; even so, we need the grace time alone with Him produces.

God Comes Looking for Me

With a certainty, if we spend too much time away from God, he is coming after us. God comes looking for me when I've let too much time between us elapse. Like a lover in waiting, I can feel him drawing me closer to him. Yet and still, I sometimes allow the busyness of my day to hinder me from answering His summons. Surprisingly, in spite of my excuses and inconsistencies, God doesn't scold me or reject me. No, he simply convicts my heart, guides me to truth, and prepares a place for me in the bridal chamber.

Beloved, God calls us to his side for a purpose. Spiritual impartations, washings, and cleansing, must be done in private. It is not done in the open where others can mock or misinterpret our entreating. God is kind as he takes us to the secret place, the intimate place, to deal with us. Thus you will never be disappointed if you submit to his will and go with him behind the veil—even if it is for disciplinary purposes. Unlike any other, Christ tenderly embraces us as he gently comforts us and prepares us for grooming, fellowship, and spiritual impartation.

Koinonia is a word in the Greek that means "fellowship, social exchange, communication, or participation." Regardless of your gift, you cannot grow and develop effectively outside of the fellowship of God. You must be connected to the vine where you can continually receive nourishment and spiritual hydration. How do you think you're going to reach your expected height of achievement in ministry without being connected to God?

As a result of being in his presence, your ministry will produce good fruit—love, joy, peace, patience, goodness, meekness, and kindness. It's quite commonly understood that we need wisdom, discernment, and insight to follow God in ministry. Therefore, if you abide in him, he will surely abide in you. When the Lord desires to make an impartation in us, whether it's to promote us, elevate us, chasten us, or cultivate us, he calls us to join him in the secret place in the presence of the Holy of Holies. That is where inner healing begins. In time, impartations spun and matured in the secret place are reflected publicly for everyone to see.

Our degree of spiritual intimacy is parallel to our degree of commitment to God in prayer, meditation, and the reading of the word.

Becoming Intimate with God

Why would the God of the universe want to know me intimately? Not in the sense of making my acquaintance, but to know me as in intimate fellowship—to actually know and even care how I feel. This is a principle Christians occasionally forget. Perhaps we think God, like man, is slack in his promises, but this couldn't be farther from the truth. God has always desired intimacy with mankind. In fact, that was his sole purpose for creating us in the first place—so that he could interact with us, and we in turn could experience and learn of him. The Jewish idiom for intimacy or intercourse is the word *ginosko*. *Ginosko* denotes the kind of passionate exchange Paul spoke of in Philippians 3:10 when he said, "That I may know Him, and the power of his resurrection, and the fellowship of his sufferings, being made conformable unto his death."

Paul wanted us to recognize that we cannot understand the essence and the power of the cross if we do not have an intimate relationship with God. The passion that scopes and defines your ministry is parallel to your ability to identify with Christ's suffering. In other words, when we are able to endure the weight of affliction, it is a sign that we have identified with his suffering. Overall, we know that situations in our lives either draw us to Christ or drive us away. However, the comfort released in prayer keeps us firmly adjoined to Christ and helps us to build a strong and powerful testimony. No one in their right mind has intercourse with somebody they don't know! The exchange is pointless; it has no meaning or essence because there is no binding attachments, no commitment—no covenant.

Christ has made a covenant with us. He has promised us love, protection, and peace in exchange for our sacrifice and willingness to obey him. Therefore I surmise as I wholeheartedly concur with the Apostle Paul that the glory is far greater than the affliction. Second Corinthians 4:17 says, "For our light and momentary troubles are achieving for us an eternal glory that far outweighs them all."

Can you make this declaration of faith? Affliction in exchange for glory! Christ's ministry cost him everything—even his life—and the joy and pain he experienced, you will also be expected to share. Through this intimate exchange, your passion is heightened, releasing a force in you to preach and execute the gospel with great conviction.

My passion to preach is fueled in knowing that God is my friend. No matter what subject I preach on, if I remind myself that God is my friend, I'll make myself happy. Why? Because God was my friend when I didn't have any friends. I grew up somewhat of a loner. I'd play for hours alone with my dolls—chatting and conversing with God. Soon he became my closest friend. Therefore, the very idea that God is my friend links heaven and earth together for me. What is God to you? Is he a deliverer, a healer, perhaps a counselor or comforter? Whatever he is to you, you will preach to others from the roots of revelation and reality he has manifested in you.

Why We Need to be Alone with God

Why do you need to be alone with God? It's simple; you can't survive without his presence in your life and ministry. Undoubtedly, God offers me more than I could ever put in a book. He is omnipotent, the sovereign giver of life, and without him, I know I can do nothing. In fact, I'm totally dependent upon his wisdom, mercy, and grace. Without God's endless display of compassion in my life, I cannot fulfill my responsibilities as a friend, mother, wife, preacher, or any of the other roles I'm required and expected to play. Apart from his presence, I'm physically, emotionally, and spiritually depleted. Do you get the picture? For me, my relationship with Christ is not optional. I must have his presence in my life. Beloved, I sincerely understand what David meant when he said, "Lord, please don't take your Holy Spirit away from me" (Psalms 51:11, NIV). You see, this goes beyond business (e.g., contesting God for a sermon to preach or a prayer that needs answering); it's personal.

Spiritual devotion and meditation is personal and should never be cumbersome or taxing. In fact, it should be quite rewarding, resembling the solace you experience after a warm cup of herbal tea, or perhaps the rejuvenation that accompanies a Saturday evening nap. It's quiet time, working-out-your-own-salvation kind of time. And though your special time alone with God may offer you something completely different from what my special time alone with God offers me, it's still a necessary ingredient to your life's existence and your ministry's advancement. All in all, you simply can't afford to neglect this fellowship.

Your Ministry Suffers when You Are Depleted

Unfortunately, preachers everywhere are burned out. They are operating on overdrive—overworked and under prayed. Consider this chilling fact. (I personally had to learn this lesson the hard way). You cannot give what you do not have. If you have failed to let God empower you in the secret place, you're not going to be able to get in the pulpit and muster up an anointing.

Some preachers try to "do" or perform ministry aside from a consecrated lifestyle. What usually happens is one ends up relying on emotionalism, gifts, and talents as a means of activating the moving of the Holy Spirit. Beloved, the anointing of God cannot be manufactured, nor can it be bought or duplicated. People know when it's "live and when it's Memorex." The intimate moments you spend alone with God will produce a genuine anointing in your life and ministry. It is the unction to function or the power to get results. But greater still, it is proof that the presence of God is actively moving and operating in your life. When a believer is dripping with the anointing of God, devils run in terror. I want demons to respond to my commands as though they were hearing directly from God. Paul had both the authority of God, and the anointing (or the presence of God) actively at work in his life and ministry. The demons in the book of Acts recognized it and acknowledged him by name.

Lady preacher, hold on to the anointing. The anointing will keep you from being crushed under the weight of ministry. Not only that, but it will calm your natural spirit so the Holy Spirit can have and maintain preeminence.

Review Precepts

1. God requires us to spend quality time alone with him on a daily basis.

2. God will reveal himself to you if you'll take time to join him in the secret place.

3. Only the anointing can help you carry the weight of ministry.

4. The anointing is birthed on the threshing floor of sacrificial prayer, fasting, and supplication.

5. Learn to value and appreciate the time you spend alone with God.

Waiting Is Gain

*T*here is a painful undercurrent to the title "Waiting is Gain." So, what does "waiting is gain" actually mean? And how does waiting effectively produce gain in the life and ministry of a believer? Well, for the answer, let's explore the life of a familiar Bible icon, Moses. His story, above many others, teaches us a very valuable lesson in the school of waiting.

Most of us are quite familiar with the accounts of Moses's life. However, for those of you who are not, Moses was a one-time prince of Egypt who was banished into exile for killing an Egyptian overseer who mistreated a fellow Hebrew. Now, when we observe this story from a panoramic view, it would seem Moses's reaction to the Egyptians' assault was a bit extreme. Nevertheless, who would argue the fact it signifies Moses's depth of passion and concern for the survival of the Hebrew slaves?

We can fully understand why God called a man like Moses to lead the people of Israel out of bondage and slavery. Moses was a man of relentless passion, and passion is the fuel that ignites purpose in one's life and ministry.

In conjunction, passion must be balanced by a tamed and docile spirit. If not, one is merely an accident waiting to happen. Beloved, this is truly the art of waiting. When passion and zeal are able to embrace patience, the gains of waiting are manifested in the likeness of a spiritually mature vessel.

Are You Prepared for Service?

Year after year, God was watching and waiting. After Moses's season of immaturity and pride had ended, God came looking for him. Imagine how he must have felt as he sheepishly covered his face from the sight of the burning bush. He riddled God with multiple questions as he doubtfully made excuses for his fears and human frailty. "Lord, what you're asking me to do is too great for me. Who is going to believe me anyway? Is there like no one else you could possibly ask? What am I supposed to say if they ask me who sent me?" Poor Moses! Did he really not know from the day of his inception God was holding him in waiting? It would seem Moses would have known that his season of preparation started long before he met God on Mt. Sinai. As a matter of fact, before Moses was even born, God had sealed his destiny. Every time he was rejected, ostracized, and ridiculed, God was making and creating a man of purpose. As an infant, his mother put him in a papyrus basket and floated him down the Nile River to save his life from Pharaoh's decree, but little did she know she was fulfilling the divine purpose God had ordained for his life. Truly, it was more than his life she saved that day. It was an entire people and the destiny of an entire nation.

The impeding circumstances of Moses's life served as a threshing floor to prepare and condition him for the challenges and responsibilities ahead. Although the plan may have seemed ambiguous and unclear in the beginning, God wanted Moses to learn how to trust Him in waiting. Beloved, everything isn't always revealed to us in black and white. As a matter of fact, God unveils the details of the blueprint at will little by little, here a little, and there a little, and by doing so, he disables us from puppeteering the plan and/or plotting to manipulate and control his will. In the midst of it all, Moses's ministry was hidden beneath the pains and agony of his youth. Every experience, both good and bad, played an essential part in the overall providential plan of God. Now, what God was teaching Moses during the interim phase (from their initial meeting on Mt. Sinai to the confrontation with Pharaoh), would require him to capitalize on everything he had previously learned and experienced.

While Moses waited for God to introduce him to his finest hour in ministry, he was forced to humbly face his fears, insecurities, and doubts. In time, it soon became apparent that Moses had given God permission to work on his heart and refine his character. By the time he finally stood before Pharaoh, he had waxed strong in spirit; faithful, bold, confident, and regal. Moses passed the test! During his vulnerable season of waiting, God had taught him how to completely trust and rely on him for the miracles and supernatural wonders yet to be manifested in his life and ministry (refer to the entire book of Exodus for further study).

Deep down inside, well beyond the topical fears, I too wrestled with the call to ministry, chiefly because I didn't want to disappoint God or make a fool of myself if I failed. And, though I eventually conceded to the call, I had the what ifs in a major kind of way. I just couldn't understand God's reasoning for choosing me! Nevertheless, there was another surprisingly strange paradigm at work within me. This perhaps being the most deceiving contrast of all, though I was afraid and uncertain about the call to ministry, I assumed because I was schooled in church activities (singing in the choir, ushering, teaching Sunday school and children's church), I was equally qualified to preach. *Not!* Consequently, nothing but the gains of waiting can adequately prepare you for the responsibility of preaching. Why? Because preaching is more than flowing in a gift; it is the characterization of a fully submitted heart. I soon found out that *come* didn't mean go; it meant wait and wait patiently.

What Am I Supposed to Be Doing while I'm Waiting?

> Lead me in the truth, and teach me: for thou art the God of my salvation; on thee do I wait all the day.
>
> Psalms 25:5 (KJV)

I've heard it said, "There is a secret to waiting." Perhaps there is; I don't really know. But one thing I'm sure of: waiting is painful. Nevertheless, God knows something about waiting we mortals don't quite understand; waiting is also gain. Generally speaking, it is in the seasons of waiting God introduces us to ourselves. He confronts us over unresolved issues and faithfulness to prayer and consecration. You must embrace these matters if you want your ministry to operate effectively, with efficiency, fortitude, and precision. God's nature must be fully developed in you. One thing is certain; maturity takes time. You advance in time-paced increments, not overnight.

Unfortunately, we live in an instamatic society. We want what we want when we want it with an immediate response and satisfactory results. Consequently, the world's system has programmed us to think this way. Thanks to global synergy and cyberspace, we've become accustomed to sending messages around the world in a matter of minutes. The faster the technology goes, the faster we tend to go. It's no wonder we expect God to operate the same way. But, just in case you didn't know it, he doesn't. The scriptures tell us that "Jesus Christ is the same yesterday and today and forever" (Hebrew 13:8, NIV). It also says, "For a thousand years in your sight are like a day that has just gone by, or like a watch in the night" (Psalms 90:4, NIV).

God lives outside of time and space; therefore, he alone sets the parameters that border our destiny. If we are totally submitted to God's plan for our lives, we don't have the option of choosing how we determine our years. God's time table is not debatable. We must choose to line up with his plan and follow his command. After all, doesn't he know what's best for our lives? I venture to say we don't always act as though we do.

Bottom line, our times and seasons are predestined by God, and we must submit to those changes and respect his will. Spiritual seasons are much like natural seasons; they change. We can't avoid it or dismiss it. Therefore, we must learn to appreciate it and enjoy the experiences that season alone affords.

As you go from one season of ministry to the other, you'll find yourself wondering while you're sitting in your waiting pattern, *What am I supposed to be doing? What do I do while I'm waiting for my springtime to come?* Well, this is your golden opportunity to put on some things and put off some things—to get alone with God and define the full scope of your ministry. Isaiah 40:31 says, "But they that wait on the Lord shall renew their strength; they shall mount up with wings as an eagle; they shall run, and not be weary; they shall walk, and not faint" (kjv). Our strength is renewed as we wait "in Him." Not just wait *for* Him, but wait "in Him!" Ironically, you gain spiritual momentum as you wait for spiritual increase.

There are some basic principles of waiting you must learn once you have gone into a waiting pattern. First of all, you should know that God will test your willingness to obey him. At any rate, one of the most essential elements of waiting is your ability to trust him. Without trust, you will not be able to patiently wait on the Lord's promise. Sorrowfully, you will succumb to intolerance and begin to entertain the voices in your head, encouraging you to move out before your time.

Ultimately, you end up removing yourself from God's line of discipleship. Once that occurs, your only recourse is to take another lap. In short, you subject yourself to a process the military calls "recycling." I'm told that troops who foul out somewhere during the first six weeks of boot camp are recycled and sent back, possibly (depending on how bad the offense) to week one, the beginning. What a stiff penalty to pay for insubordination. Unfortunately, at some point in time, we've all had to undergo the shame and disappointment of recycling, simply because we've failed to follow God's instructions. Nevertheless, "spiritual recycling" is wantonly painful. Yet I'd venture to say in most cases, it's often avoidable.

The Trust Factor

God knew I could not effectively do ministry in my own strength, so from the very beginning, He taught me how to stay put and to rely and depend on Him— exclusively. The Holy Spirit encouraged me to divert the temptation to build a ministry on my own human efforts, gifts, and talents.

Like most people, frustration, discouragement, troubles, and testing will either force you to lean on your own human attributes or solely on the infallible arm of the Lord. In every obstacle, trail, and setback that I've personally experienced, God allowed for my spiritual increase. Understand it's simply a part of the process.

This is where trust is manifested; so it is each time an individual is spiritually promoted. God requires him or her to be ready and willing to advance to the next level or degree of faith and commitment. We go from "faith to faith" as we go from "glory to glory." Moreover, we grow in faith as we wait in patience. God will not give you spiritual promotion until your faith catches up to the glory. For instance, as my faith began to grow and I began to trust God for the level of glory he was taking me to, I was able to rest and patiently embrace the process of transformation. "But let patience have her perfect work, that you may be perfect, (mature) and entire, wanting nothing" (James 1:4, KJV). Waiting became much more bearable as proof of my spiritual increase began to manifest.

Beloved, we must grow up and mature in patience. Ministry is not for the immature! In fact, patience is one of the most valuable lessons to be learned in ministry. Without it you are going to be a poor listener, supporter, and leader. Waiting gives you the privilege and opportunity to exercise patience and develop maturity. David said, "I waited patiently on the Lord; and he turned to me and heard my cry" (Psalms 40:1, NIV).

Perhaps one of the most important aspects of the waiting pattern is learning how to be sensitive to God's voice. A preacher who is unable to distinctively differentiate the voice of God from that of Satan or man is in very serious trouble. How will you ever be able to rightly divide the word of truth if you cannot understand and discern the leading, guiding, and spiritual utterance of the Holy Scriptures? This is how lying prophecies and error infiltrate the church—ignorance. In your season of waiting, take advantage of the opportunity to glean revelation and understanding of the scriptures. You must ask God for the ability to observe, interpret, and apply the scriptures accurately—to exegete. Read your word daily and familiarize yourself with the art of memorization. If possible, go to school, but at any rate, make every effort to learn the Word of God through study, meditation, and prayer.

Paul was not a sluggard but a scholar who aggressively studied the scriptures. How else would he have been able to write over half of the New Testament? All in all, he was qualified to preach the gospel of Jesus Christ. In a similar way, you too must be qualified to lead others. We will discuss this issue in detail in chapter nine, entitled "Blind Leaders."

Setting the House in Order

> Surely you desire truth in the inner parts; you teach me wisdom in the inmost place.
>
> Psalms 51:6 (NIV)

Believers have learned to make excuses for their inconsistencies by hiding behind pointed scriptures. Needless to say, it is a futile effort. Eventually evil squatters will possess the un-surrendered territory in your life and destroy your ministry. God is a discerner of the heart, and he knows everything about us. We can't, even on our best day, fool him. As God meticulously reveals us to ourselves, we must be willing to allow him to chasten and correct us. We know God is merciful. It is evident by the fact he doesn't sentence us to what we really deserve. Nevertheless, we must trust him with the chastening process.

I define chastisement as the art by which God manually shapes, molds, and forms us into usefully viable vessels. Beloved, it's true; if you launch into ministry before God has chastened and refined your character, you are subject to ruin everything he has ever promised you. It's your choice. But I warn you in advance, you will not have the fortitude to stick and stay if your character cannot support the weight of your ministry. Perhaps in your free time you can do a short study on vessels of clay. Learn how they are made and the process they go through in order to become a viable instrument. Then compare it to the developmental process of a spiritual metamorphosis (Jeremiah 18:1-6).

Undoubtedly, we must be made into the image of God. Whether you are a preacher or not, you must renounce worldly affections completely. I'd venture to say if you truly belong to the family of God, you'll do whatever God requires in order to destroy the affections and appetites of the flesh. Flesh cannot be permitted lordship over the will of Christ in your life. We were born with sinfully inherent desires (iniquity). The Bible says we were "shaped and fashioned in iniquity" (Psalms 51:5, NIV). Therefore, it takes time and a willingness to change in order to get free and stay free from worldly lust. This is especially true if you have entertained sin (flesh sins in particular) for an extended period of time.

Worldliness and lust don't just go away. Your season of waiting allows you uninterrupted time to deal with the overt and covert indiscretions in your character before you stand before God's people. "Those who belong to Christ Jesus have crucified the sinful nature with its passions and desires" (Galatians 5:24, NIV).

Perhaps you're wondering, *How do I do that? How do I free myself from the bondages of the flesh?* Well, plain and simple, you must be delivered. Listen, there are times we have to cry. Further still, we occasionally have to bitterly travail, actually purge ourselves on the threshing floor of repentance until true freedom comes. That's what I had to do when God was chastening me—bitterly travail. "During the days of Jesus' life on earth, he offered up prayers and petitions with loud cries and tears to the one who could save him from death, and he was heard because of his reverent submission. Although he was a son, he learned obedience from what he suffered" (Hebrews 5:7-9, NIV).

Comparing myself to Luke's account of the woman with the alabaster box, my tears represented my sincere love and gratitude to God for healing, delivering, and saving me. "I loved much because I had been forgiven much" (Luke 7:36-50, NIV). In fact, I earnestly wept before the Lord until my living room couch began to resemble a mourner's bench. Sometimes I prayed for days on end. Before long, my tears became a sign of obedience, purging, release, and surrender. You too will experience freedom if you will permit God to thoroughly wash your spirit. Of course, that is oftentimes easier said than done. Yet, when God starts taking things we want away from us in order to groom and mature us, it requires nothing less than total submission.

Available to Serve

Ministry today is extremely challenging. There are multiple programs and activities that need manning—most of the time by volunteers. No doubt it is every bit a full-time job, and some pastors absolutely expect a full-time level of productivity and commitment from you. I'm not talking about quality time; I'm talking about quantity time—time away from your home and family. When I was growing up, pastors actually did all the work in the church: preach, pray, turn on the lights and heaters, sweep, mop floors, and visit the sick. But today, pastors are moving toward *body ministry* by placing more and more responsibility on the team. Depending on the size of the ministry, lay ministers may be expected to have experience in a variety of areas—anywhere from presiding over the service to facilitating a study group. Consequently, if you have issues in your personal life that have become a menace and a strain on your mind, time, and money, then ministry will only compound it.

Stop and take an inventory of your life. Are you in debt? Do you have poor spending habits? Do you desire to finish school and haven't done it yet? Are you struggling with relationship issues? Are you in poor health? While you are in your waiting pattern, you need to begin to make some positive lifestyle changes so you don't start off your ministry hindered by personal problems.

Down through the years, preachers have preached against Christians like "busy Martha," Lazarus' sister. But, honestly speaking, everybody can't be like Mary, sitting around at Jesus feet. Somebody's got to work. We must pray that the Lord of the harvest will send laborers into the fields to help us. I assure you it is impossible to minister effectively if you are not mentally, emotionally, spiritually, financially, and physically healthy and balanced. Instead of you being an asset to the ministry, you'll eventually find yourself becoming a deficit.

So handle your business! If your problem is financial, be a good steward. Stop spending, start saving, and stop running from your creditors. If it's relational, confront the individual(s), repent, forgive, and reconcile; whatever it takes to repair the breech. Beloved, you want to free yourself to minister without unnecessary weights. You will be much more effective in ministry if you use this season to do that. Listen, I could give you numerous suggestions on how to put your life in order, but you must be willing to walk it out if you are ever going to see productivity. "In the same way, faith by itself, if it is not accompanied by action, is dead" (James 2:17, NIV).

You, Your Family, and Your Ministry

Did you know you fulfill your duties to God when you care for your home and family? "Notwithstanding she shall be saved in childbearing, if they continue in faith and charity and holiness with sobriety" (1 Timothy 2:15, KJV). Sad to say, but I have known lady preachers who've aborted their families to answer the call to ministry. And though I strongly support empowerment, I do not believe God wants women to sacrifice their families for the sake of the ministry. It may, however, seem difficult to do, but you can effectively support the ministry while limiting your availability to the ministry. Of course, I recognize the dynamics of this subject is vast, as there are many reasons for the choices one has to make concerning their subsequent roles in ministry. Nevertheless, there must be a reasonable balance whereby the basic principles of family responsibilities, duties, and commitment apply.

Without the loving support of my husband and children, I would not be able to do what I'm doing today, at least not comfortably. My husband has always encouraged me to maximize my potential, whether it concerned my career, education, or ministry. He has always been my greatest supporter, and equally important is the support of my children. I've always said, "I didn't want to save the world and lose my own children." We have five children, and sometimes they think having dual pastor parents is cool. But, like all kids, they require a lot of time and attention. Rarely, if ever, will either my husband or I accept an invitation without first checking the family calendar. We both recognize the importance of being actively involved in our children's lives. So to avoid conflict, we converse with the family first. We are partners; therefore, we work together to support both the ministry and our parenting duties.

Married in Ministry

Ideally, every married woman who answers the call to ministry will have a supportive husband and family. However, this is not always the case. If this is your position, prayerfully and respectfully communicate your calling to your spouse. Talk to him in a language he completely understands: respect. And, if at all possible, avoid using church slang, especially if he is not yet a believer.

First you need to be honest with him regarding your calling and encourage him to accompany you in the journey. Incidentally, as a result of your call to ministry, he is, in some way or the other, also called to ministry. That, of course, poses new challenges, expectations, and responsibilities that may appear stressful or overwhelming to your spouse. Perhaps you should ask him, "How do you feel about my call to ministry? Does my calling affect how you perceive our roles? Questions like these must be addressed. Even basic questions need not be overlooked. Issues such as how many nights a week you're going to be out of the house, if you are going to be expected to travel or spend extra money, and who will be taking care of the house and the children while you are away.

Now, ladies, don't get upset and lose your composure. These questions are valid and deserve careful consideration. In most families, women are still expected to be homemakers, even if they work outside of the home. Regardless of whether your husband is saved or not, you want the two of you to be in agreement. Though he may not be able to cover you spiritually, as your husband, he can support you and cover you naturally. If there is no agreement, there is no support. Perhaps in time he will be ready to discuss his feelings about your calling. When he does, try to allow him to do so uninterrupted, without interjecting or responding with condescension, criticism, and/or sarcasm. Reassure him that you will never use the pulpit or a "sister girl meeting" to say mean and ugly things about him behind his back.

An unsaved husband fears his wife will put his business in the street and make him look like a devil in front of the church folk. Remember, if you disrespect him at home, he won't believe you when you tell him you don't disrespect him at church.

If you find your spouse is consistently resistant to your call to ministry, don't fight and argue about it; investigate it. Go to your knees in prayer and petition the Lord for understanding. Get to the root of the matter and declare war! Not against him but against the enemy. First, ask yourself this simple question. "Why is my husband so defiant?" Directly or indirectly, we know Satan is the problem. However, if you look a little closer, you may find he is not as much to blame as you may have previously expected. One of the primary reasons men become frustrated with women in the church is because they abuse or breach their promises. For instance, you may have agreed to limit your time away from home to two or three nights a week, yet without notice or a reasonable apology, you consistently violate that promise. Or perhaps you have become delinquent in your regular domestic responsibilities in the home (especially cooking), and/or you've gotten into the habit of making excuses for your failure to minister to his personal needs. All these acts of inconsideration give place to the enemy.

Single in Ministry

> I wish that all men were as I am. But each man has his own gift from God; one has this gift; another has that. Now to the unmarried and the widows I say: It is good for them to stay unmarried, as I am. But if they cannot control themselves, they should marry, for it is better to marry than to burn with passion.
>
> 1 Corinthians 7:7-11 (NIV)

Contrary to popular belief, singleness is not a curse. In fact, everyone should know there are both advantages and disadvantages of being single. Though some of you may be single by choice, others perhaps are not. Nevertheless, if you learn how to be content as you patiently wait for change, Boaz will eventually come. Of course, being patient while waiting is not a guarantee you are going to find a mate. What if it is not God's will for you to be married? Will you be able to be content with His decision for your life? At any rate, patience will make the journey much more palatable—whichever way the pendulum swings.

Nevertheless, if you desire to be married, and that is indeed an honorable choice, make your request known to God and labor in the ministry as you wait. Whining and complaining will never force God to move any faster. If you are overly anxious and consumed with lust, you are going to forfeit your Boaz and settle for Bozo. Nobody said it was going to be easy, but you have got to trust God and wait for the promise. Bozo is waiting for you to become exhausted as a result of waiting and gleaning in the fields, and once he recognizes your state of weariness, he'll rob you of Boaz and eventually highjack your future. Maximize this season in your life by building upon your own assets. God already knows the thoughts and plans he has for your life. The question is, do you? If you find your purpose for existing, you will discover networks and resources that are available to help you reach your personal goals and move you toward self fulfillment.

"I would like you to be free from concern. An unmarried [wo]man is concerned about the Lord's affair—how [s]he can please the Lord" (1 Corinthians 7:32, NIV).

Being Found in God's Favor

Some people may equate the pains of waiting with the lack of favor. The plausible conclusion if favor ain't fair is to assume that some people have the favor of God and others do not. Perhaps it's easy to understand how someone could make that mistake, but nothing could be farther from the truth. Just because you don't look like you are experiencing a favorable season does not mean you are not prospering. Everyone, whether saved or unsaved, has a season for reaping tangible blessings. Yet I've learned how to find value and worth in every season in my life. Part of the waiting process is having the confidence of knowing God is blessing you even though you may not be able to visibly measure the growth externally. Closed doors are often misconstrued. Saints, we don't always know why the doors in our lives are shut—especially when we have been faithful to prayer and fasting. But as strange as it may seem, you're in the right place; don't get discouraged. God is making an honorable leader out of you. Therefore, he will hold up certain areas in your life and ministry until you are ready to be released. Listen, Jesus told his disciples he was sending them out as lambs among wolves. But he didn't send them out before they were ready to go. Surely you don't want to be fodder for the enemy, do you? Then remember, closed doors during this season of waiting will teach you to trust him, release control, and sow today for tomorrow's harvest.

Consider these biblical attributes: faith, love, patience, goodness, meekness, kindness, self-control, perseverance, and godly character. All these attributes, my friend, are signs of God's inner favor. Contrary to popular opinion, true spiritual growth is not measured by tangible possessions. True spiritual growth is learning how to rest in the waiting pattern. When you know your season is coming and you're patiently waiting for God to open or close certain doors, you know without a doubt you are in his favor.

Can you give God permission to open and close the doors in your life at his command? If you can trust him with the remote control to your life, you will grow by leaps and bounds. I knew I had grown in God when He'd closed doors to employment opportunities and unfruitful relationships in my life and I did not reason or complain to Him about it. Consequently, if we respond favorably to God's opening and closing the doors, we will actually be experiencing His divine favor. Simply put, we are in God's favor when we are in God's will, and the world will see the manifestation of his favor (in our lives) in his time. Beloved, I tell you the truth: there are times when I'm discouraged because the doors of opportunity do not open when I think they should. However, through prayer and love I don't have to pick locks or force my way in; I know God will make all things perfect in His time.

Somebody Please Give Me the Microphone!

> Unless the Lord builds the house, its builders labor in vain. Unless the Lord watches over the city, the watchmen stand guard in vain.
>
> Psalms 127:1 (NIV)

Though waiting is difficult to do, those who refuse to wait on God frustrate themselves and their leadership. At times the desire to demonstrate your gifts takes precedence over God's spiritual training and sound reasoning. When leadership refuse to give way to these men and women and they cannot get visibility during the general assembly, they'll rally an audience the best way they can—regardless of the medium. In some churches, testimony service is subject to turn into "preach offs," as impatient preachers lay privy to the glory and the microphone. Sad to say, but these preachers are preoccupied with nothing less than scoring points. They've lost focus on winning souls, unity among the brethren, supporting the leadership, or celebrating the manifestation of the presence of God in the house.

All they want is the microphone. "A gift opens the way for the giver, and ushers him into the presence of the great" (Proverbs 18:16, NIV). I like the way it reads in the King James Version: "A man's gift maketh room for him, and bringeth him before great men."

When my husband was in the military, I discovered an important fact: nobody in the church gets seniority.

Every time you move to a new location, you go to the back of the bus until a place is made for your gift. Please understand that God uses whomever he chooses, whenever he chooses. We don't know what the house needs from week to week. As a matter of fact, the pastor doesn't even know. That's why we pray for God to give us a right now word. Our objective is to see God's presence fill the temple.

Too many preachers are restlessly waiting for their turn to preach. Either they are pressing their lips together in disgust or pushing their way to the front as they trample upon the sheep. At any rate, instead of working in the fields, they are agitating the environment. The work of the Lord is plenteous, and if preachers get out of the pulpit and go to the fields, the world will see an influx of souls for the end-time harvest. Have you been called to the fields? You must go to the fields, my friend. The fields are wherever you are needed to work, in spite of your passion and calling.

Review Precepts

1. Waiting is the scale that balances passion and zeal.

2. Waiting is inevitable. It's God's way of proving your character.

3. In order for patience to have her perfect work in you, you must endeavor to trust God right where you are.

4. Only after you've willingly permitted God to chasten and refine your character will you witness successful (productive) gain.

5. Maximize the waiting season by putting yourself in a position to serve, study the word, and support the ministry...wherever and whenever possible.

6. As a wife and mother, your first ministry begins at home.

7. Singleness at times is lonely; however, marriage (at times) is equally lonesome. Do not look on either side of the pond and lose yourself in a field of dreams. Don't become a seeker of nebulous ambitions and/or self-pity. Stay focused on the promise and be content in whatever state you are in.

Pulpit Etiquette

How, then, can they call on the one they have not believed in? And how can they believe in the one of whom they have not heard? And how can they hear without someone preaching to them? And how can they preach unless they are sent? As it is written, "How beautiful are the feet of those who carry the good news!"

Romans 10:14-15 (NIV)

*O*ften times the preacher is under tremendous pressure to perform. Everyone has a different opinion of how she is supposed to preach, what she is supposed to look like, and how she's to conduct herself.

I saw my first popular lady preacher many years ago while attending a meeting in Dallas, Texas. When she came through the double doors of the hotel ballroom, the audience immediately gave way to the hush of silence. Mesmerized by her grace, we all gazed upon her. Her silhouette was that of a princess. None of her outward features struck me as poetic, yet she was angelic is appearance. Meanwhile, as I found myself basking in the serene moment, the lady preacher joyfully approached the hour-glass podium. Sweeping the dimly lit room with her compassionate eyes, she single-handedly bowed her head and quietly gave homage to the Lord in prayer. To my surprise, she made (what I thought) was a shocking statement. "Although I've stood before audiences many times before, each time still feels like the first. Beneath my chaste exterior, my palms are sweating, and my knees are knocking. Nevertheless, the call to duty awaits me."

I took notice as she conquered her human frailties and fell into the arms of grace. "Umm," I replied. "Wow, she is human, just like me!"

Consequently, the first rule of ministry is learning how to relax and find solace in your new position. Somehow you must ascribe to define your own ministry. Perhaps the essential task is discovering what actually works for you. Once you determine that, you will be able to fairly critique yourself, improve your pulpit delivery, and better your overall style and performance. Well, it's a challenge, but as my momma used to say, "Never let them see you sweat."

Preparing to Preach

I will begin by saying this: preaching involves both spiritual and technical skills, and preparation is ultimately the key and driving force behind your continual success. Going before the audience unprepared is bad business and a bad habit to formulate. If you are well prepared, you will be able to conquer many of your natural fears. For instance, you should arrive at your destination on time so you can receive instructions, familiarize yourself with your whereabouts, and discern the spiritual climate. Do you have your bible, notes, or other supplies and materials? Where do you need to meet for consecration and prayer? At all costs, you want to try to eliminate unnecessary anxiety by taking care of simple necessities like these before you get to the pulpit.

Whereas technical skills are important to master, spiritual skills are of greatest benefit to you as a preacher. Therefore, whether your primary strengths are natural or spiritual, you never want to get into the habit of relying on your ability to work your gifts as a means of demonstrating or exhibiting a successful presentation.

Yes, we should give God glory for the messages we preach, but don't forget the fact that he is using your mouth and brain to channel the word to the people. We automatically bring a part of ourselves to every scripture, song, and sermon we preach. In fact, everything we do has a fraction of our own human element attached to it. Why? Because we are human— we are not divine. Therefore, you want to be as confident as humanly possible with yourself, your message, and your presentation without compromising the authentic word from God. This will enable you to decrease self and minister with boldness and conviction.

If you combine your technical and spiritual skills together, your overall delivery will be greatly enhanced. In case you were wondering what I consider a natural skill, it is first and foremost the skills you were not only born with, but may have learned in a basic college speech course. For instance, you should have learned how to stick to the subject, perform good eye contact, use the proper enunciation of words, and to cautiously minimize the use of slang and/or other unfamiliar terminology.

In most cases, when one is preaching, she has to consciously take notice of her use of these natural skills. Note such questions as, "Am I looking at the audience or staring up at the ceiling? Am I turning my back against the audience, obstructing their ability to understand what I'm saying?" All of these things are considered natural or learned skills and can in part be mastered over time.

Unlike technical skills, spiritual skills are often utilized subconsciously. Beyond that, if spiritual skills are accompanied by the anointing (the presence and approval of God), they will usually present themselves involuntarily, instantaneously, and without contemplation. There are three points I'd particularly like to take the time to highlight. They are not a means to an end, but they are indeed profitable for pulpit success:

1. Become very knowledgeable and familiar with the text. Who are the characters involved? What do you know about the character's lifestyle and history? Did you exegete the text appropriately? Is your interpretation accurate?

2. Identify with you audience. Are you realistic? Can the people "get with you?" Are you able to

make the scriptures applicable to the people's needs? Does your personal character reflect the positive aspects of your message?

3. Converse with God. Have you spent adequate time alone with God in prayer? Are you dripping in the anointing? Or, are you stale and lifeless, fishing for a spiritual signal?

Identifying with Your Audience

> When they see the purity and reverence of your lives...your beauty should not come from outward adornment, such as braided hair and the wearing of gold jewelry and fine clothes. Instead, it should be that of your inner self, the unfading beauty of a gentle and quiet spirit, which is of great worth in God's sight.
>
> 1 Peter 3:2-4 (NIV)

As a woman of God, you set the example for women everywhere you go. It doesn't matter whether you preach the gospel or not. As a Christian woman, you should strive to consistently demonstrate the beauty of holiness. People are always watching you and looking for imperfections in your character, appearance, attitude, demeanor, and personality. Like it or not, people judge you based upon these criteria. So ask yourself, "What do people see when they look at me? What kind of impression do I leave on the minds of onlookers?"

First and foremost, people want preachers to be real. Far too long we have preached what we ourselves have not tried to live, and the sheep have blatantly lost confidence in our self-imposed images. Bottom line, people will abhor your ministry if they question your character. Think about it: how do you convince people over the pulpit that you're holy and righteous when your reputation and demonstration reveals otherwise? If people see you mistreating others, lying, committing adultery, stealing, gossiping, causing dissention, etcetera, then you'll never whole-heartedly obtain their respect no matter how hard you try.

If you have the respect of your audience, you can make a textual mistake, and people will earnestly pardon. For instance, most people know David not Joshua killed Goliath. But if you lack integrity, people will hold that against you and rightly so. One thing is certain: there is sweet consolation in knowing that your heart is pure and your hands are clean. Then and only then can you truly become one with your audience. When you have nothing to hide, prove, or protect, you can face your audience with a clear conscience and a heart to serve.

To reiterate this principle, consider Eli's and Samuel's sons. Notwithstanding the fact these men were preachers (born of the Levitical order of priests), sin kept them from getting close to the people. They irreverently desecrated the temple and the sacred oracles, confiscated the money, and caroused with the women, and the people lost respect for them. These boys were wicked, having lost their lives, their families, and the Ark of the Covenant because of their immoral and presumptuous ways.

Another important factor for you to consider when identifying with your audience is recognizing the dexterity of relating genuine love and impassionate sympathy for the needs of the people. Quite commonly, people want to feel loved and cared for, and preachers will eventually lose their connection to the people if they are unable to feel their parishioner's needs. In most cases, the congregation's biggest concern is whether you, the preacher, genuinely care about the condition of their souls. Coincidentally, any time you see church portrayed on television, movie preachers before, during, or after the service are somewhere in the foyer, greeting the people and embracing the little children. Beloved, this is a natural expectation.

Although certain factors may indeed prevent you from physically touching everyone within your congregation, your pulpit demeanor will relay your heart's intent, that's for certain. Masses of people followed Jesus everywhere he went because he had a reputation of meeting their holistic needs. Regardless of the severity of their issues, he never sent them away empty handed nor empty hearted. Jesus had compassion for the needs of the people both naturally and spiritually. People today still want a spiritual leader that will take the time to minister to them on a personal level. Unfortunately, the mega-ministry craze has almost wiped the one-on-one pastor-people relationships out of the church. Preachers in general are spending less and less time with the flock, and that is not always a good thing.

Appeasing the People

It has become more and more difficult for preachers to comfortably preach against the doctrine of sin. Certain stake holders will pressure you to water down your message to avoid what they call "offending others." Paul told Timothy in 2 Timothy 1:11, "And of this gospel I was appointed a herald and an apostle and a teacher. That is why I am suffering as I am. Yet I am not ashamed, because I know whom I have believed, and am convinced that he is able to guard what I have entrusted to him for that day." Consider this: how do you keep from offending others when you're preaching against their sins? Simply put, you can't. It's totally impossible.

Jesus offended people all the time, especially the pious religious leaders. In fact, even his own disciples left him when he began to entreat them to submit to God and die to the flesh. When people don't want to adhere to the truth, they will say as those disciples said to Jesus, This is a hard saying, who can hear it (John 6: 53-61, NIV). Jesus had to tell the disciples, having known the rebellious nature of their hearts, "Will you leave me because I tell you the truth?" (John 6:41-66, NIV).

If you preach the truth and people become disillusioned, angry, or unsupportive, there's absolutely nothing you can do about it. Shake the dust from off your feet. Consequently, whether you preach the truth in love or in indignation, you must be prepared to lose a few. In the example text, the word says, "and the disciples walked with Jesus no more." Regardless of who is offended, you'd rather suffer persecution in the will of God than bow to the knee of man. We live in a day and time where people have itching ears. They want to hear what pleases the flesh, and no matter how far left or right you may venture, somebody somewhere is not going to like it. So you decide whether you're going to please God or try and please man. Nevertheless, if you faithfully preach the word of God, not philosophy, anthropology, or any other ideology, those who want to be set free will hear the word of the Lord and obey.

Jeremiah was a young man when he began his ministry in Judah. God told him straightaway not to look upon the people's faces. In doing so, God said he would become discouraged and disheartened. I suggest you and I also follow God's advice. The countenance of the people will distract you. As a matter of fact, if you're a discerner of hearts, you'll be able to study their faces and know exactly what they're thinking, and they won't have to say a word. Yet if you're not careful, their intimidating stance will cause you to faint and ultimately lose heart.

Nevertheless, if you're comparing the validity of your ministry by the *hallelujah*s and *amen*s of people, you're going to be terribly disappointed. People change allegiance very quickly. God is the one that endorses your ministry, so don't rely on people's responses as proof of acceptance. If you preach the word of God with boldness and conviction, the anointing will follow, and escort with it signs of approval.

Selecting Sermons: What Should and Should Not Be Preached or Shared across the Pulpit

> The Spirit of the Lord is on me, because he has anointed me to preach good-news to the poor. He has sent me to proclaim freedom for the prisoners and recovery of sight for the blind, to release the oppressed, to proclaim the acceptable year of the Lord's favor.
>
> Luke 4:18-19 (NIV)

To define *passion*, you'll frequently hear me utilize such words as *sincerity*, *conviction*, or *zeal*. Perhaps I'm a bit redundant, but I can't seem to help myself. I'm simply convinced that a man without passion is a man without purpose. Passion will ignite one's faith and ministry by propelling her to move beyond her own personal ideals and beliefs in order to embrace a sound proclamation of spiritual truth. Your testimony is an example of that depth of passion and truth.

Aside from God putting his words in your mouth and guiding your hands to the appropriate scriptures, your testimony serves as a witness to your faith. The Bible says in Revelation 12:11, "They overcame him by the blood of the Lamb and the word of their testimony and they did not love their lives so much as to shrink from death." Your testimony is a byproduct of your passion. Furthermore, it never becomes ancient or outdated. It always has the power to overcome the enemy and solidify your faith—even the faith of those who hear it.

In addition to your testimony, selecting appropriate material to preach is a matter of meeting God's divine appointment. I have previously alluded to the fact that only God knows what the people need. He knows who is attending the meeting and who stands indecisively in the valley of decision. Therefore, it is imperative that you approach the scriptures in prayer. Ask God, "What do your people need to hear today?" Remember, canned, boxed, and re-processed sermons will not suffice. God's people always need fresh manna, a right-now, not-yesterday kind of word.

The church today goes through many fads and trends. Sometimes preachers ignorantly seize the rhythm of the movement and find themselves drifting off course, far away from the great commission. But balance is the key. Moreover, I believe pastors should be informed, educated, and conscious of the pertinent issues that affect our world, issues such as foreign affairs, church-related legislation, and news of public interest. Thus, if we are not ignorant of Satan's devices, we will not perish at the hands of his deception. Just the same, Satan (purposefully) specializes in sidebars and rabbit trails—anything to entice you to direct your energies away from the word of God and onto subjects and projects that are exhaustive and futile. In consequence, one of Satan's most reliable weapons against the church is distraction. Distraction is a plausible ace in the hole. It is, by far, a reliable weapon against the modern-day church.

Nevertheless, we have a responsibility to exegete the scriptures so they come alive, relative to the people and the problems of today. Paul successfully bridged the revelation of Christ with the current issues of his time. Your messages should also reflect the two. However, I can't stress enough how important it is to stick with the Word! If you preach the Word, you will not be tempted to rant and rave over issues that do not produce life or provide adequate growth and increase.

Honestly speaking, if you don't know what to preach, I'll give you some good advice. Preach the kingdom of God. Jesus preached about those things that pertained to the kingdom—salvation, faith, love, forgiveness, wholeness, the authenticity of the Godhead, unity, etc. He didn't preoccupy himself with Caesar or the traditions of the Pharisees. His objective was to preach the good news of the gospel. Certainly God will give you what he wants you to preach. But, rest assured, if you rebel, causing your messages to lack balance, hearers may conclude that your ministry is confrontational and controversial.

Again, everything should be balanced by the word of God. Overemphasizing (for or against) any one thing will cause your ministry to become unproductive and ineffective. Those who subscribe to your ministry will assume your preoccupation with any or all of the identified topics are a cover up for a lack of self-confidence, personal involvement in sin, or a means of compensating for true Bible knowledge and/or an authentic calling. The list below contains a selection of topics I've labeled unfavorable. However, you be the judge:

- Attacks against the congregation.
- Overkill on political issues.
- Obsession with issues of an immoral nature.
- Stating support for or against radical, fascist movements.
- Persistent attacks against other leaders (outside of your congregation).
- Promoting selfish agendas.
- Broadcasting your spiritual conquest.
- Startling the audience with shocking, vulgar, crudely comical, or inappropriate words or statements.
- Denominationalism and ritualistic traditions.
- Over emphasizing prophecies and spiritual gifts.
- Forming an alliance with the world or yielding support for the artifacts of the world.
- Trying to conceal covert attacks against specific people (within your congregation) during your messages, testimonies, etcetera.

- Poorly disguising confidential information within your sermons (revealing other's personal business).

- Hateful semantics for particular groups, formal and informal.

- Gloating over personal achievements, commemorations, and assets.

- Openly discussing your own personal business, especially information about your spouse and/ or children.

- Constantly re-visiting attacks against your person.

Of the topics mentioned above, it is important to note that women, more often than not, abuse issues of a personal nature. Perhaps in most cases preachers do not purposefully intend to attack, mislead, or confuse the sheep. However, preachers are no different from anyone else. They too can be hurt and/or misunderstood. Yet if they fail to deal with their issues in prayer, the enemy will use it as a trap against them.

Bottom line, hurt people hurt people, and divorcing your emotions from your ministerial duties is sometimes difficult to do. Due to the church's design and culture, it's an unfortunate portal for persons to "speak their mind" and "have their say." Way too often, flesh supersedes sound judgment, and people are wounded and offended by the insensitivity of others.

Nevertheless, if you are broken in some specific area in your life that could cause, even by accident, an infectious outbreak to spread among the congregation, you need to quarantine yourself and obtain spiritual healing.

Always try to settle your differences before you get in the pulpit. If you do, you're less likely to slip up and say something you'll later regret.

Review Precepts

1. Take the art of ministry seriously, not half heartedly. Handle it in a professionally skilled manner.

2. Identify your assets and deficits and govern your ministry accordingly. In other words, capitalize on the assets and work on the deficits.

3. You are a woman of God, so purpose to act and behave like one. Don't misrepresent or abuse your position. It is not wise to burn your bridges.

4. Avoid preaching above your level of revelation and understanding. If you lack wisdom in a certain area, take the time to seek it out before you preach it.

5. Again, refer to the list of unfavorable topics and subject matter. It will help you in the long run.

The Cloning Effect

*F*inding your place in ministry definitely takes time. Much of what you've learned you've actually learned by observation. Most of us (if we're truly honest about it) have found ourselves acting out the antics of preachers we secretly admire. And though this may not necessarily be a bad thing, it's important for you to appreciate the gifts God has placed in you. New ministers are frequently unfamiliar with the art and skills of public speaking. Coincidentally, standing before an audience is initially frightening. However, if you're going to do it, purpose in your heart to do it right! The right way, mind you, is your way, the way God gave it to you. Though you may proudly celebrate the ministry of others (role models and pulpit icons) you must acquire an appreciation for your own flavor and technique.

When David volunteered to fight Goliath, King Saul tried to encourage him to fight in his armor, but David candidly refused. He knew he was unfamiliar with the use of Saul's apparatus; therefore, he prepared himself to fight with the skills he had acquired in the fields.

There was no question in David's mind whether he had the fortitude to bring Goliath down. But to do it, he knew he had to do it his way. So David went after Goliath with a rock and a sling. Thus with God as a shield before him, David slew Goliath, claiming the ultimate victory. Why was David so successful? The answer is simple; he trusted in his God and the skills God had given him, refusing to allow himself to become a clone of Saul. Cloning is an unhealthy interference with self-worth, self-acceptance, self-expression, and, in due course, success and victory.

Our God is a creative God, and he designed you with the power of ingenuity. You are therefore unlike anyone else. In fact, when God made you, he broke the mold. Out of the millions of people on the planet today, only you have the code to your DNA. Beloved, everything about you is unique, and that's what makes you who you are. David said, "For you created my inmost being; you knit me together in my mother's womb. I praise you because I'm fearfully and wonderfully made; your works are wonderful, I know that full well" (Psalms 139:13-14, NIV). No doubt God knew what he needed when he made you. He designed and fashioned your personality and character to accent his divine purpose. Just the same, your gifts and talents are uniquely arranged to complement his plan.

Cloning in and of itself encourages you to hide your gifts behind someone else's image, not the image of Christ. Authenticity is genuine, nothing artificial, and that's what the world is crying out for today—realism. Preachers who are sensitive to the moving of God within them have learned how to capitalize on their own strengths and abilities are without a doubt most successful in today's ministry. Jeremiah 1:5 says, "Before I formed you in the womb I knew you, before you were born I set you apart; I appointed you as a prophet to the nations" (NIV).

What Is the Cloning Effect?

First and foremost, let's define "the cloning effect." The cloning effect is an evolutionary process whereby the individual composition of one person is transformed into that of another. Webster defines a clone as "one that appears to be a copy of an original form." When believers lose themselves' in someone else's image, they soon find themselves a victim of cloning. Though no one sets out to lose their self image, factors such as low self-esteem, discouragement, and past hurts significantly affect how we respond to our own gifts and talents.

To compensate for those deficiencies there is a tendency to adopt someone else's personality and style. Fortunately since the cloning effect progresses in stages, you at any point in the transformation can arrest the behavior and recapture your own sense of value and worth. That's exactly what God is looking for!

By the way, since there is so much talk these days about "loving self" or "self-love," I want to clearly define and differentiate my use of this term. Self-love, in the context of this chapter, is not the "worship of self." It is appreciating what God has put in you (your gifts) in order to recognize, master, and utilize your own potential.

Who Are Clones, and How Are They Created?

Cloning is not a practice exclusively reserved for a Michael Jackson or Elvis Presley wannabe. Clones mirror one another in an array of fashions. Whether we are spanning the attire of a hip-hop enthusiast or that of a blood-thirsty rocker, cloning goes well beyond the exterior façade; it penetrates the psyche of an individual. Religious clones are no different from their secular counterparts. Those who have grown astutely unaware of the subtle transformation, often struggle privately to maintain or recapture their own image. It is believed that association brings about assimilation. Therefore, it is important for us to know who we are and strive to appreciate the best in others without becoming lost in their image.

If not, we stand the chance of becoming entirely void of originality and personality; becoming merely captive to the ominous power of the cloning phenomena. When this occurs, it has the propensity to overshadow the beauty and godlikeness in their Christian character.

Victoria Robinson, former president of the Protestant Women of the Chapel (PWOC) in Europe summed it up like this: "The church must strive for unity, not uniformity." There are many different reasons for cloning.

Subconsciously it may be linked to one or more of the following reasons:

1. Clones think they are following Christ when in actuality they are following a man, an institution, or an organization.

2. Clones desire to be like the people they idolize.

3. Clones usually have low self-esteem and self-worth.

4. Clones have an overwhelming need to be needed. They thrive off the rush of other's pleasure.

5. Clones admire and covet the response people give their idols' behavior.

6. Clones are afraid if they act like themselves they may not be accepted.

7. Clones haven't learned how to master their own skills; therefore, they are uncomfortable being themselves.

Walking in Jesus's Footsteps

> To this you were called, because Christ suffered for you, leaving you an example that you should follow in his steps.
>
> 1 Peter 2:21 (NIV)

Surely there are many worthy role models for us to follow and emulate, but without a doubt, Jesus is by far the greatest. Who would be a better personality to mirror than Jesus Christ? After all, Jesus is not only the head of the church but the perfect example. As we purpose to look more and more like him, without ever asking, people will know we are indeed his followers. Then there will be no need to wear an "I love Jesus" tee-shirt or an "honorary Christian badge." The traits that Jesus posseses we too will possess in increasing measure. In fact, people will look at your conduct and conclude that you are a follower of Christ. "When they saw the courage of Peter and John and realized they were unschooled, ordinary men, they were astonished and they took note that these men had been with Jesus" (Acts 4:13, NIV). Overall, people will observe your demeanor, disposition, and demonstration and ascertain your circle of association. If you've spent more time watching and learning the techniques of men rather than the ways of Christ, that's who you're going to emulate.

How can you look like Jesus if you're not following in his footsteps? You may be using his Bible and speaking his words, but are you acting like him? Jesus was motivated by the needs of people and the unction of the Holy Spirit. He was not moved by manmade cues and humanistic antics. Jesus was an original. In fact, everything about Jesus was uniquely original—his birth, his mission, and his purpose. That was probably one of the reasons he was so hated among the Pharisees. Jesus's ways continuously frustrated them because they could never ascertain the direction he was going. He was always changing his technique. On numerous occasions, he'd remind them all, "I do what my Father tells me to do, the way he tells me to do it." One day he demonstrated this statement when he spit in the mud, made mud patties, and healed a blind man's eyes with the moistened clay. Then on another occasion, he spoke life into a centurion's daughter without ever leaving the city or changing his direction.

Whether cloning affects an individual or an institution, the fundamental objective is to systematically control the operation and demonstration of the Holy Spirit. The Bible teaches us, "Thus you nullify the word of God for the sake of your traditions" (Matthew 15:6, NIV). This no doubt grieves the Holy Spirit. We mustn't allow ourselves to become fixated on a formula, program, or method. Consider the fact our God is rich in mercy, daily providing us with fresh manna. If we try to save yesterday's manna, it's going to formulate maggots and rot. In comparison, you can't put new wine in old wine skins. Fresh wine will eventually burst old skins. To be an original, you must release God to flow through you like new wine. No matter how He chooses to move, you must yield to Him. Clones have the tendency to get comfortable with methods. So comfortable, perhaps, they can't seem to recognize Christ when he manifests himself in a different format. Although Jesus Christ is the same yesterday, today, and forever, His methods and demonstrations are transmutable.

The Byproducts of Cloning in the Church

You know a church is suffering from varying degrees of cloning when the environment, culture, and atmosphere are lifeless and void of power. It exemplifies the church Paul described in 2 Timothy 3:5: "Having a form of godliness but denying the power thereof"

(KJV). Churches of this nature are not difficult to find; as a whole they are usually stagnant and unproductive. Signs of territorial disputes infiltrate the atmosphere as saints war over turf, promotions, and their idols' endorsements. Carnality takes precedence over the moving of the Holy Spirit, and, as you may very well imagine, the church is weak and hollow, void of faith and spiritual vitality. Instead of the house being fueled by love and the fruit of the Spirit, it's fueled by envy, jealousy, and every evil work.

Saints who join themselves to churches of this kind must eventually conform to the characteristics of the people therein, suffer persecution, or pack up and leave. Thus, individuals who don't fit the cloning pattern(s), are subject to being black balled or labeled a "non-conformist." The cloning effect is pernicious, and individuals who do not go with the flow are often forced outside of the inner circle and ostracized by the elites.

Why Do You Want to Be Like Mike?

I understand how the cloning effect invades one's self image. A few years ago, I was reading a web note from "Youth Noise," a column very similar to "Dear Abby," when this young lady (we'll call Sally) was complaining about the cloning behavior of her new friend (we'll call Mary). Sally began her story by saying her and Mary's relationship started off quite nicely. They enjoyed shopping, eating, and hanging out together. All of a sudden, Sally noticed Mary started to change. She began to wear her hair just like Sally's and buy identical outfits, shoes, and accessories. She even tried to monopolize all of Sally's time by imposing herself upon her and her other friends. Sally went on to say, "If Mary said she liked something and I said I didn't, she would change her mind about it, just because I said I didn't like it." In the end, Sally asked the columnist what she should do. "Mary's behavior is starting to annoy me," she said. "I could take advantage of her, but I can't."

As you can imagine, Mary's cloning behavior had not only become irritating but very tiring as well. The strain of having to carry Mary's lack of self-confidence, self-worth, and self-expression became too much for Sally to bear. Until Mary becomes a whole person, complete, and at peace with herself, she will strain every relationship she enters. Whether it is a family member, friend, or future companion, Mary, and people like Mary, look to others for ways to complete themselves. What they may or may not realize is they eventually wear out the patience of those around them.

Perhaps Mary just wanted to be like her idol, Sally. But the root cause for Mary's cloning behavior goes much deeper than identical outfits and hairdos. Mary's behavior is a direct result of her lack of knowledge and failure to appreciate her own self-worth. It all boils down to the fact that Mary doesn't know her divine purpose or her reason for existing. Therefore, she takes on the image and purpose of someone she thinks she would like to resemble and emulate.

Idols Great and Small

Webster defines *idol* as "an image worshipped as a god: an object of passionate devotion." When we begin to idolize people, we are not only disobeying God, but we are making ourselves slaves to an invisible master.

Some people will go to great lengths to be like the people they so passionately admire. They have an overwhelming desire to capture their idols features, attributes, expressions, and personality. Unfortunately, some clones will stop at nothing to seize the imprint of their idol's image. This is a very sad commentary, especially among believers. God told us to walk in His image and not that of a man. Yet we consistently promote flesh over the image of the Lord Jesus Christ. As the unified body of Christ, we have not learned how to appreciate the gifts and talents of others without getting lost in the brilliance of their image.

In every sect of society, we have seen the disruptive nature of idol worship. Just stop and take a look at the condition of our youth. Some of them have been utterly destroyed by the spirit of rebellion and lust as a result of their affections for destructively perverse, misogynistic entertainers. It's sad, but it is but one of the many examples of idol worship at its most heightened degree. Indeed, the variations are perhaps too numerous to list, both in and out of the church. But, at any rate, idol worship is a prevalent enemy of God and is prohibited by the first commandment given to Moses on Mt. Sinai. However, not withstanding honor (because we should give honor where honor is due), it is possible to appreciate and respect someone else's gift without losing yourself in their image.

Another important aspect to consider is clones will frequently put themselves on the spot to imitate their idol's methods. For example, your idol may be a handsomely groomed singer and as a ritual enjoys performing a crowd-stirring selection before he or she preaches. Realizing you, among many others, like to see and hear your idol's melodic presentation, there's a serious problem; you, for one, can't carry a note in a hand basket.

Though you have practiced singing their song in the mirror and moving your body to the rhythm of their beat, the truth of the matter remains unchanged: you've stepped outside of your naturally gifted element, and it doesn't work for you.

Rediscovering Yourself

Paul said in 1 Corinthians 11:1, "Be ye followers of me, even as I also am of Christ" (KJV). Paul encouraged believers to imitate the qualities Christ demonstrated throughout his life and ministry.

I realize I've spent a considerable length of time discussing the negative implications of cloning; however, I believe for purposes of understanding it was necessary. Nevertheless, this rainbow has a silver lining. In fact, I'd like to balance this scale by addressing this same basic idea from a positive perspective. Instead of the word *clone*, which to me raises negative impressions, we will use the word *imitate*. *Imitate* means to follow as a model, to copy, resemble, or reproduce. There is a grave difference between modeling the positive characteristics of someone who is following the ways of Christ and losing your identity and self-expression in someone else's image.

If you look closely at the definition of *imitate*, you'll find it relatively describes the characteristics of a mentor. We will discuss mentoring further in the final chapter. At any rate, every saint should endeavor to follow individuals who exemplify the attributes of the Lord Jesus Christ. Such are pastors, teachers, apostles, prophets, and evangelists, all the saints who diligently strive to imitate Jesus like the disciples in the early church.

As we demonstrate the attributes of Jesus Christ before the world and the church, the fruits of the Holy Spirit will boldly manifest in our lives and ministry. Indeed, that is a good thing and is worthy of modeling and duplication.

Finally, to break out of the cloning effect, you must first find yourself, love yourself, and receive yourself. Learn how to glean from those who have impacted your life without getting lost in the matrix of the cloning effect. Remember, authenticity is genuine, nothing artificial.

Review Precepts

1. You are a designer's original, and you're calling is genuinely authentic—again, nothing artificial.

2. The cloning effect is defined in this book as an evolutionary process whereby the individual composition of one person is transformed into that of another.

3. Clones allow themselves to become systematically controlled and/or programmed by the actions or behaviors of others.

4. Break out of the cloning effect by defining and rediscovering your purpose.

The Other Side of Ministry

*M*inistry has an ugly side. Reports of clergy misconduct serve only as a reminder of the ill-marked examples of the current condition of the Christian church. Though it may be difficult to discuss and even harder to accept, scandal and spiritual looting is prevalent throughout Christendom today. Too often, preachers sequester and censor the rotting truth that festers behind closed doors.

Whereas hiding has always been a common response to sin, we can only heal what's revealed and brought to the light. The Bible says, "Men love darkness rather than light, because their deeds are evil" (John 3:19, NIV). Nevertheless, it is imperative that we the *ecclesia* take off the mask and tell the truth—at least among ourselves. Whether the painstaking paradigm comprises the teachings and practices of a conservative Episcopalian or that of a liberal Baptist, the fundamental malign remains unchanged. We have an enemy, and his name is Lucifer. Satan has not changed his course of direction. It's still written in John 10:10, "The thief comes only to steal and kill and destroy; I have come that they may have life, and have it to the full." Satan knows he cannot curse the church, nor can he prevail against it. But he can cause the church to curse and condemn itself, and that's exactly what he has set out to do—to entice us to condemn ourselves.

Perhaps I should warn you in advance that the next three chapters in this book will primarily address the problematic issues that affect the livelihood of the Christian church. This chapter in particular will identify a segment of problems frequently underestimated in terms of its probable potentiality to incite internal destruction. These are disagreement and conflict, dealing with offenses, unforgiveness, haters, the spirit of competition, loneliness, and the spoils of success.

Who Is the Church?

First and foremost, let's define the church. What is a church? And who are its members? Webster defined the church as a place of worship, the Lord's house, or the whole body of Christians. Moreover, the leading definition describes the church in the context of a place, a building, or a set location. But the church is more than a place; it's a people and a Christian community of believers.

Paul also described the church as a body, categorizing the whole in parts, with each individual part (the head, the eye, the foot, etc.) representing or collectively comprising the whole. Thus, Paul was pointedly emphasizing the concept of "oneness."

Christ is not coming back to redeem independent parts, an arm here or an eye there. No, he's coming back for a body (singular), a church defined without spot or wrinkle.

As a minister of the gospel, you must realize that the church today is not in its perfected form. The church is a viable organism subject to systemic problems and illnesses. Yet she is still the bride of Christ and a mighty army of believers authorized by God to shake kingdoms and bind and loose spiritual forces. In short, we are an extension from his ascension though at this time we are literally under construction.

The Price to Follow Jesus

> If the world hates you, keep in mind that it hated me first. If you belonged to the world, it would love you as its own. As it is, you do not belong to the world, but I have chosen you out of the world. That is why the world hates you. Remember the words I spoke to you: No servant is greater than his master, if they persecuted me, they will persecute you also, if they obeyed my teachings they will obey yours also.
>
> John 15:18-20 (NIV)

Jesus never said securing the succession of the church would be easy. Ministry requires total sacrifice. Are you willing to pay that price? When my husband and I lived in Japan, we witnessed first hand the cost of following Christ.

Over the course of about five years, we saw many Japanese people give their lives to Jesus Christ. Yet the Japanese reluctantly receive and accept Christianity as their primary religion because they know what converting from Buddhism to Christianity could possibly cost them. You see, Japan practices a national religion; therefore, when the Japanese convert from Buddhism to Christianity, their families will often reject them. These Asian converts are blatantly accused of committing treason, not just against the family and the ancestral pedigree but against the culture, the society, and in some cases, even the nation. In fact, some of them have lost everything to follow Christ, yet they did so without reluctance or remorse. Even today, amongst great opposition, they remain steadfast in the faith.

Perhaps many of you reading this book may never be required to make such drastic sacrifices to follow Christ. But one thing is certain: you will make some. At almost every level of ministry, most of the problems you encounter will involve interfacing people, other members of the body of Christ. Because you are in the people business, you are going to experience people problems. Your job is to learn how to successfully manage those problems. In a most immediate way, you must ascertain the skills to interact and communicate with people, all people, even difficult people, without jeopardizing your convictions, integrity, or witness. No doubt if you fail to master this feat, your ministry will greatly suffer.

Disagreement and Conflict

> Therefore, if you are offering your gift at the
> altar and there remember that your brother has
> something against you, leave your gift there in
> front of the altar. First go and be reconciled to
> your brother; then come and offer your gift.
>
> Matthew 5:23-24 (NIV)

No matter how gracious, sensible, or professional, people and personalities sometimes clash, causing working conditions to become severely strained. Tension will emerge not only from the external sources without but from the internal sources and conflicts within. Human nature compels you to fight to the finish. Soon, pride faithfully cheers in delight, egging you on and daring you to stand your ground. It's a tug of war, and the battle is between the enemy and your flesh. It may be hard to believe, but people are not the enemy; although, in reality, they may very well be the dupe that's causing the problems. Nevertheless, Satan is the accuser of the brethren, and it is he who stirs people to propagate conflict. Paul encourages us to live at peace with all men.

Whatever the cause, conflict is uncomfortable. Whether we label it "irreconcilable differences, conflicts of interest, or strictly intolerance," it has the power to destroy the fabric of a ministry.

Nevertheless, if conflict becomes too difficult to manage, a separation agreement should be warranted. At almost any rate, it is better to separate yourself from the environment (peacefully if at all possible) than to stir up strife and dissention among the brethren. In a similar way, disagreement and conflict caused Paul and Barnabas in Acts 15:35-41 to separate. They did not, however, separate as enemies but as fellow believers with the overall health and welfare of the church in mind.

Perhaps of greatest importance is the practice of reconciliation. We must always consider first the benefits of reconciliation (I'd say above all else). Reconciliation is one of the most significant principles in the word of God. No doubt, we are here today because Christ offered his life in exchange for us. Beloved, if we can reconcile with our offenders, we've not only won our brother or sister, but we've also diverted the trappings of Satan by releasing ourselves from the snare of offense and the root of bitterness. The net result: if we profess to be Christians, exercising love and patience, though we separate, we should try our very best to forbid our differences from permanently damaging one another's spirit. We must consistently follow the scriptural guidelines found in Matthew 18:15-17 (NIV):

> If your brother sins against you, go and show him his fault, just between the two of you. If he listens to you, you have won your brother over. But if he will not listen, take one or two others along, so that every matter will be established by the testimony of two or three witnesses. If he refuses to listen to them, tell it to the church; and if he refuses to listen even to the church, treat him as you would a pagan or a tax collector.

Of course, this scripture does not give us permission to stop loving or praying for our offender(s). No, it simply permits us to let go of the offense and move on. Ideally, respect for one another, a sincere desire to promote harmony and peace among the brethren, and a compassionate concern for the desolation of the sheep is more than enough to spur mature saints to resolve unnecessary dissention.

Dealing with Offense

Probably one of the best books I've ever read on offense was written by John Bevere, *Bait of Satan*. In reality, offense is the response one takes to a disdained violation, and unforgiveness is the result of that accepted response. Bevere makes the principles of offense quite easy to understand by comparing offense to cheese on a mousetrap or meat in the snare; unforgiveness and bitterness will patiently wait for you to bite. Once you've taken the bite, you're immediately caught in the snare. If you can avoid the offense, (not necessarily the conflict) you can avoid the trap. Again, conflict is inevitable, but we can choose whether or not to take an offense.

In theory, that sounds well and good. But what do you do if you've already been caught in the snare of the trap? That's a good question; however, the answer is quite simple. You pray! Ask God how you should best release yourself from the sting of the offense. Do you need to confront the individual(s)? Or do you need to release them in prayer?

First, you must allow God to deal with your heart and clarify the facts of the offense. Do not allow yourself to pause in modes of repeat, rehearse, and rewind. Remember, Satan frequently magnifies the issues by misconstruing the facts. For instance, here is a common precursor to a typical offense. It's the final phrase before the trap snaps. "Did you see what she did? She's got her nerve. How *dare* she say something like that to me!" "I knew it! She's never really liked me anyway." If you're not very careful, at that precise moment, you could find yourself embracing, actually harboring, an offense—possibly over a false assumption.

Immediately, stop and exhale. Then ask yourself a few questions. "Is there a possibility I've misunderstood what was said?" or, "Is what I heard actually what she meant?" Seek the counsel of the Holy Spirit and never confront people or issues when your emotions are running high. You should know by now that Satan will put people in your path to help you foster the offense. That's his job. If he can keep you in bondage, he can prevent you from being an effective witness.

In retrospect, there were several incidences in my life—hindsight being twenty-twenty—when I would have been "slow to speak and slow to wrath." As the Bible says in Matthew 10:16, "Be ye therefore, wise as serpents and harmless as doves" (KJV).

Saints, I've had many opportunities in my life to harbor offenses. Yet I realized early on that my response and subsequent reaction to offense would either build my faith and ministry or completely destroy it. Thank God, in spite of myself, the Lord "delivered me from the snare of the fowler."

How Do I Forgive?

Jesus said in Mark 11:25, "And when you stand praying, if you hold anything against anyone, forgive him, so that your Father in heaven may forgive you your sins" (NIV). Unforgiveness is like a blemish on the heart of God's people. It barricades love, prohibiting it from freely flowing. I realize forgiveness is not always easy, and the more ominous the offense, the more difficult it seems. Yet one man in history knew better than most the struggle one encounters to forgive their enemies. His name was Joseph.

As a result of his brothers' jealousy, Joseph was sold into slavery, accused of a crime he didn't commit, and eventually sentenced to solitary confinement, yet he was a man of impeccable character. He refused to become a slave to the master of offense. In time, God gracefully rewarded him for his integrity by elevating him to a kingly position.

When Joseph's brothers returned to Egypt in search of food and materials, they didn't even know he was alive, let alone commissioned as second in command to Pharaoh. Joseph, staring directly in the face of his violators, had the power to get revenge. By the time he was ready to reveal his identity, love had changed his heart. Perhaps to the astonishment of some, Joseph earnestly loved his brothers in spite of what they'd done to him. So it was when the moment of reckoning presented itself, he could do nothing more than weep and say, "What you meant for evil, God has meant for good." Although Joseph had every reason to be callous and unforgiving, like you and I, he didn't have a right to withhold forgiveness.

Beyond Joseph's encounter with forgiveness is the story of our beloved Savior, Jesus Christ. His is the ultimate test of forgiveness. Christ looked down from the cross of suffering and empathetically forgave his executioners by saying, Father, forgive them for they do not know what they are doing (Luke 23:34, NIV).

In as much as lies within you, you must practice forgiveness. Yes, the process is painfully agonizing. Nevertheless, we have been commanded to do it. "Not just seven times, but seventy times seven" (Matthew 18:22-23, NIV). I'd venture to say if it were not for pride, forgiveness in many cases wouldn't be such a complicated task. Nevertheless, we are without excuse. "Love your enemies and pray for them, for in doing so, you will heap coals of fire on their heads" (Proverbs 25:22, NIV).

Haters: Dealing with Jealousy and Envy

The Bible is filled with crimes of jealousy and passion. David understood the sting of jealousy and hatred. Saul, David's father-in-law, hated him because he knew God had chosen him to be the next king. David was loved among the people, loved among the women, and loved among Saul's house, and he couldn't stand it. In fact, he chased him all over the plains of Israel trying to destroy him. The psalms clearly support the fact that David's heart was wounded as a result of Saul's jealous aggression.

Lady preacher, this may or may not come as a surprise to you, but you are going to be wounded by people in ministry—leadership, laymen, and comrades alike. Depending on the severity of the offense, you may be tempted to seek revenge, demand restitution, or simply "give somebody a piece of your mind." But if you don't control your urge to retaliate, you'll find yourself becoming a hater.

Perhaps you're wondering, "How do I become the hater if I was the one who was violated?" Well, when you foster and rehearse the offense, either in word or deed, you are sowing seeds of hate. Haters hate over the simplest of things; it doesn't have to be anything big. Don't feel bad. Regardless of the circumstances, it all boils down to this simple fact: people either love you or hate you…oftentimes without a sensible cause—that's just the nature of the beast. Don't take it personally. Just move on!

Every time someone becomes envious over something they themselves wanted or thought they deserved, a hater is born. Jealousy is a spiritual seed, and it can germinate very quickly, rapidly giving way to hate and even to murder (Genesis 4:1-14). Miriam, Moses's sister, was stricken with leprosy after jealousy began to defile her ministry. She went to her brother

Aaron, complaining about Moses and his wife: "'Has the Lord only spoken through Moses?' they asked. 'Hasn't he also spoken through us? And the Lord heard this'" (Numbers 12:2, NIV).

I adjure you, check yourself and make sure you're in the right spirit. Jealousy and disdain can flood your emotions before you know it, but stop it in its tracks before it becomes a major stronghold.

The Spirit of Competition

One of jealousy's greatest supporters is the spirit of competition. As a matter of fact, competition is astutely birthed out of the spirit of jealousy. In the world's sector, incentives are used to coerce and encourage advancement and competitiveness among highly motivated personnel. Sometimes the competition is good, and sometimes it's not. But at any rate, I regret to announce that competition in the church is of no exception, and unfortunately, it seems to be growing at an alarming rate. Instead of men measuring themselves by the word of God, they measure themselves by themselves, and Paul said this was not a wise practice (2 Corinthians 10: 12). Overall, it initiates jealousy and envy by encouraging preachers, as well as other leaders, to compare their gifts, talents, and number of followers. Far too long we have confirmed and qualified one's "blessings" by quantitative measurements. Yet material possessions have never been an accurate tool to measure and validate success. Success is achieved when an individual discovers and eventually maximizes their true God given potential.

In the end, it's all relative; relative to God's plan, that is! Talents are issued on the basis of our God-given abilities not in accordance to our dreams and aspirations. God alone divides our portion, and in spite of what we think we deserve, he knows what we can and cannot handle. The old folks used to say, "Your eyes are bigger than your stomach." Nevertheless, if we maximize the number of talents we are given, whether we define them as great or small, we will begin to see ourselves as stellar performers. Then there will be no need to look at anyone else's tally as a means of qualifying personal success (Matthew 25:14-28).

Set your own benchmarks. If you don't, you're going to see others succeed and become miserably discouraged. God only holds you responsible for what he has given to you.

When You Feel All Alone

It is not uncommon for depression to accompany victory. While some are rejoicing over the pennant, others are overwhelmed by post-war fatigue. Tragically, some preachers leave the pulpit every Sunday morning inspired and encouraged, and by Monday afternoon they are entertaining thoughts of failure and futility. Perhaps you may find this idea rather outlandish, but consider the story of Elijah the prophet. He is a perfect example of post war fatigue.

Elijah challenged and defeated the prophets of Baal during a showdown on Mt. Carmel. Shortly after racing past King Ahab on the desert plains, he discovered the king had promptly arrived at Jezreel, only to cowardly inform his wife Jezebel of Elijah's heroic doings.

In her fury, she sent Elijah these pernicious words: "May the gods deal with me ever so severely if by this time tomorrow I do not make your life like that of one of them." Afraid, alone, and embracing self pity, Elijah sits underneath the Juniper tree, "I have had enough, Lord," he said. "Take my life; I'm no better than my ancestors" (1 Kings 19:4, NIV). Read all of chapter 19; it will truly inspire you.

Yes, it does seem strange, but this great prophet of God was depressed. Elijah had overwhelmingly convinced himself that he was the only one standing up for righteousness. What an assumption! It stands to reason why he would feel so discouraged. The thought of doing ministry solo would discourage any preacher. God is an excellent strategist, and though he may use you mightily, you'll never be the only righteous leader. God will always have a faithful remnant. In fact, God told Elijah, "I have seven thousand prophets besides you who will not bow their knee to Baal," (1 King 19:18). Beloved, Satan is crafty; he knows if he can't defeat you by confounding your faith, he'll discourage you, and you in turn will defeat yourself. The enemy is at his very best when he is able to isolate you from the fellowship of other believers. Don't fool yourself, you're a much easier target to strike when you're wandering in the pastures alone.

Consequently, you were not purposed to walk independent of fellowship and support. The stressors of ministry may indeed force you into hiding—that I understand. But God asked Elijah while he was waddling in his depressed stupor, "What are you doing here?" (1 King 19:9, NIV). Perhaps when we find ourselves in a state of self-pity, we should ask ourselves that same question. Discouragement will (not might) come, but God is still with us and for us. We need only to remind ourselves of that simple promise. "He will never leave us or forsake us" (Hebrews 13:5).

In the first book of Samuel, David and his men returned to Ziklag only to find their encampment had been destroyed by the Amalekites. As you can imagine, David's men were furious, desiring to kill him as restitution for their wives and children. But David encouraged himself, got alone with his God, and prayed for wisdom and instructions. He went after the Amalekites with the attitude to "pursue, overtake and without fail recover all" (1 Samuel 30:8, NIV). Much like David, you may not have the support you need when you need it. Instead of people helping you, it may seem as though their trying to kill you. Nevertheless, if you learn how to encourage yourself, you will not fail for fear of loneliness, discouragement, or despair.

Mishandling the Spoils of Success

Finally, concerning promotion and success, I once heard Joyce Meyers say, don't let your gift take you where your character can't keep you. How true! Whether you possess an authentic anointing or not, people frequently follow gifted people. In spite of character flaws, charismatic preachers are still inspiring and attractive to onlookers. Friend, success in the wrong hands is like a loaded revolver; if you don't know how to handle it, pull the trigger, and it will handle you!

Although gifts may come without repentance, don't be deceived. It's not wise to misuse and take advantage of God's grace. Saints, consistently monitor your character for undetected flaws and inconspicuous errors. Understand it is the little foxes of lust, pride, and self-righteousness that will ultimately destroy your vine.

Beloved, there is a grave danger in operating gifts aside from repentance and righteousness. Case in point, do you remember the story of Samson? In this biblical example, Samson was the Nazarite judge whom God anointed to deliver the Israelites out of the hands of the Philistines. Although Samson was always getting into trouble, God had anointed him, moving mightily in his life and ministry. Yet, irrelative to God's mercy and grace, Samson mishandled his anointing by boasting in his "feats of strength" and chasing "sexual conquest (1)." In the end, it became apparent that the pleasures of his flesh meant more to him than the author of his calling, and he tragically died alongside his enemies—perhaps in victory but ultimately in disgrace.

As we embark upon the next chapter, we will discuss in detail the damaging effects of Balaam and the lust for power, money, and fame. In brief, we should never compromise our integrity for instant gratification. Balaam was a prime example of mishandling the spoils of success: "Woe to them! They have taken the way of Cain; they have rushed for profit into Balaam's error; they have been destroyed in Korah's rebellion" (Jude 11, NIV). And also, 2 Peter 2:16: "But he was rebuked for his wrong doings by a donkey—a beast without speech—who spoke with a man's voice and restrained the prophet's madness" (NIV).

Review Precepts

1. The church is not a perfect entity. Though she is currently under construction, she is destined to obtain perfection.

2. The dark side of ministry is often hidden from the general public. In addition, many leaders regretfully succumb to the realities of ministry and the tyranny of church related scandal.

3. Wherever there are people, there are problems. Leaders however must learn how to successfully manage such issues.

4. Forgiveness is not an option; it's a command.

5. Jealousy is a spirit and a natural response to competition. That's why Paul ardently abhorred it.

6. Oftentimes spiritual depression is a symptom of burnout.

Welcome to Holywood

*P*erhaps you are familiar with the legendary tale of Doctor Faustus. Faustus sold his soul to the devil in exchange for money, sex, and power. Though Faustus may have been a fictitious character, the moral implications of this tale were by no means fictitious—nor were its fateful plight unimaginable.

In Matthew 4:1-11, Matthew shares Christ's encounter with temptation as we find him in the desert having fasted forty days and forty nights. According to the commentary notes of the Life Application Bible, scholars suggest for temptation to be successful it must be fundamentally based on a "real need" (1535). Ironically, Satan not only tempted Jesus at the point of his real need, but also with every recourse he had available to him—*the lust of the flesh, the lust of the eyes, and the pride of life* (1 John 2:16, NIV). Nevertheless, let's look at this story a little closer, observing in detail Satan's triplex effort to strategically offset Christ's honor, integrity, and duty.

First, Satan (unsuccessfully) attempted to attack Jesus where he was obviously most vulnerable—in his physical body. He knew Jesus was hungry. Forty days and nights is a very long time to go without food and water. The degree of hunger Jesus was experiencing at this point in his fast was either "eat or die." Yet when that method of temptation didn't work, he tried to appeal to Christ's emotions. "If you are the Son of God, throw yourself down; surely God will protect you. Aren't you God's son? What a shame, your Father has left you out in this desert to die. You're hungry, thirsty, and all alone! Perhaps you should test His true love for you." Satan's temptation limpidly implied that Jesus was forgotten, unloved, and unappreciated by his Father, a trick commonly played on mankind today. At any rate, Jesus wasn't buying it, and, of course, Satan's plot failed again. But as fate would have it, his taunting wasn't over yet. Once more, Satan attempted to trip Jesus up. This time he arrogantly approached him using the alpha dog of all temptations. "I'll give you everything this world has to offer if you will bow down and worship me." What! Worship Satan? Yes! That's the very thing he wants the most, our worship. Satan understands the power of worship; therefore, he will offer us things, just about anything we want in exchange for our worship. In consequence, it is the desire for those things (money, sex, and power) that ultimately brings us to the foot of Satan's altar.

When the World Gets in the Church

History concurs with the scriptures, as it yields proof that there's nothing new under the sun" (Ecclesiastes 1:9, NIV).

Since the beginning of time, man has been tempted to sell his soul in exchange for worldly ascendance. Today people everywhere are destructively in hot pursuit, in search for the illusion of the American dream. In the words of the hip-hop rapper 50 Cent, their aim is to get rich or die trying. The Bible says, "The eyes of men are never satisfied" (Proverbs 27:20, NIV).

With each passing day, the appetites of the world become pervasively intolerable. In fact, we shouldn't even expect unsaved men to honor the moral laws of society. Don't you know unregenerate men will do just about anything to apprehend the pleasures of the flesh? After all, they are merely behaving like their father, the devil.

It is no secret; that is the way of the world! But, saints, it should not be the way of the church. The church is supposed to respond to temptation and worldly acclaim in the same manner Jesus did; "For it is written." There is a serious problem, a conflict of paradigms, as the spirit of the world is now in the church, and the church has responded inappropriately by opening her arms to embrace the spirit of the anti-Christ. Throughout the New Testament, Paul distinctively identified the characteristics of the world and the characteristics of the Spirit. Consequently, there is absolutely, emphatically, no similarities. He encouraged believers to "crucify the flesh and walk in the Spirit" (Galatians 5:17-26). Perhaps it may seem strange to ask, but how does the world get into the church if the church is in the Spirit?

It is a well-known fact that the church is not a perfect entity. It is a hospital for wounded and broken people. However, God is holding leaders everywhere accountable for the church's condition. Although Adam at the birth of creation gave the world and its power to Satan, Christ at the cross—en route to the resurrection and ultimately to the throne room of God—reinstated our authority. Yet we are still being victimized by immoral decadence, both outside and inside of the church. Quite naturally, it would seem fitting to accuse Satan for the current condition of the Christian church, but in reality, we can't—at least not conclusively. In actuality, Christians, and especially Christian leaders, have failed to deal with the sins that are rampant within their own personal lives, not to mention the sin that is diffused throughout the body of Christ.

There is a spiritual principle that supports this phenomenon. It is called the principle of transference. In Psalms 133:2, the Bible speaks of the oil that flowed from the head of Aaron the priest, down to the skirts, and upon his feet: "It is like precious oil upon the head, that ran down upon the beard, even Aaron's beard: that went down to the skirts of his garment" (NIV). Taking this scriptural text into consideration, I would venture to say whatever drips from the crown and the beard of the leaders will eventually penetrate the awaiting congregation. Whether the substance is indicative of the oil of the anointing or of the sins of the Father, it has the potential to stain the skirts of the garment. This is the net result: If leaders are sick and diseased, how can they expect the congregation to be spiritually well? This is a perfect example of follow the leader. As the leader goes, the people go (carefully take the time to read all of 2 Peter 2). Leaders are required to set the example by exemplifying Christ-like behavior.

Love of the World

> Then I will give you shepherds after my own heart, who will lead you with knowledge and understanding. Jeremiah 3:15 (NIV)

Have you ever wondered how true Christian believers could become so infatuated with mammon? Not just mammon or money, but power, position, and status as well?

Look around you. Ministry today has drastically changed. The focus of the church has shifted. Things we do in church today would have never been done twenty or thirty years ago. And though evolution is praiseworthy, I fear we have progressed beyond our commission. It's sad to say, but some Sunday morning services resemble a commercialized clip from *Lifestyles of the Rich and Famous* as shepherds great and small ardently desire to emulate the pomp and status of worldly success. Even the poorest of preachers are sporting fancy clothes, luxury cars, and bodyguards. To our horrid disgrace, the ritzy persona of Hollywood has desecrated the sanctity of the Christian church.

Everybody knows Americans love their celebrities, and celebrities in turn love the tremendous amount of capita they gross as a result of the people's affections. Loyal fans will purchase anything and everything their favorite celebrities market: books, perfume, clothes, movies, CDs, etcetera. Outwardly it appears that a large majority of Hollywood's elites covet and worship the Benjamins. Much like Hollywood, "Holywood" celebrities and elites equally crave the glory that money, visibility, and notoriety affords.

I fear some preachers, if offered the opportunity, would mirror the decision of Faust and sell their souls to the devil to experience the luxury of Holywood.

The god of this world has blinded the minds of many of our spiritual leaders. In fact, the enemy has masked their spiritual sense of discernment and reasoning, causing them to succumb to the lust for attainment. One thing is certain: preachers of this liking want to make it big, irrelative to the cost. But as you may well know, politically induced positions don't come cheap. A preacher who toils to become rich and famous will eventually be forced to compromise his or her message, *and*, in time, his or her integrity.

The irony of it all lies in the fact that people today have options. They can hear who and what they want to hear and support who and what they want to support. Consequently, the Bible clearly warns us that "in the last days, men will have itching ears, seeking out teachers that will pleasure their senses" (2 Timothy 4:3, NIV). In addition, the scriptures go on to say, "They will not even put up with sound doctrine."

Therefore, if you refuse to preach what the people want to hear, they will turn you off and find someone who will. Of course, that is a serious problem if the livelihood of your ministry is dependent upon their financial support. Everyone knows that messages such as prosperity and blessings, double portions, seed-time and harvest sell much faster than messages that voice intolerance for sin, holiness, and the power of the blood.

Jesus asked Peter as they sat by the Sea of Galilee, "Peter do you love me? Feed my lambs. Peter do you love me? Feed my sheep" (John 21:17, NIV). Perhaps the question for the Peters of this age is not whether you will feed his sheep but whether you'd rather be fed than feed the sheep.

Saints, pastors, and preachers today are intoxicated by the love of money. Some preachers have chased every kind of fad imaginable, yearning to increase their number of followers. Over the last few years, it has become apparent that many of the flagrant expressions of "spiritual" manifestations we're witnessing in our churches today are not originated by God, but rather the desires of the flesh. Strange fire! Gimmicks!

Preachers everywhere are creating ways to control, manipulate, and puppeteer the sheep. Such leaders are feigned and deceiving, as they perpetrate before the flock a lifestyle of holiness. When in reality, it's an attitude of affectation. That's the emulated source. These men and women employ a spirit of false humility and total insolence.

Seeking Power

> Woe to shepherds who are destroying and scattering the sheep of my pasture!" declares the

Lord. Therefore this is what the Lord, the God of Israel, says to the shepherds who tend my people: "Because you have scattered my flock and driven them away and have not bestowed care on them, I will bestow punishment on you for the evil you have done, declares the Lord."

Jeremiah 23:1-2 (NIV)

Power cradles the rich. Therefore, to possess power is to produce wealth. Kingdoms have come to ruin and nations have been utterly destroyed, not for freedom or the right to proclaim liberty but for the lust of a few men with a craving to control others. Moreover, for many years the spoils, profits, and benefits of power have pervasively outweighed the "greater good" (true benevolence). Some Hollywood celebrities have candidly admitted that power is addictive. If you think about it for a moment, it was power that Lucifer craved as he worshipped before God in heaven and power Eve envisioned as she contemplated eating the forbidden fruit.

The fall of the entire human race evolved from one impassionate point: "The lust of the flesh, the lust of the eyes, and the pride of life" (1 John 2:16, KJV). The lust for power is not discriminating. Power attracts everyone whether they are rich or poor, black or white. Power struggles can formulate out of nowhere; yet they can and will spread just about everywhere—the church, your home, your job, you name it. It's amazing, but even toddlers will scream and throw temper tantrums until they get what they want. Unbeknownst to them, they've learned how to use manipulation to obtain control and possession.

Unfortunately, the lust for power and the need to control and manipulate others is a problematic issue within the Christian church. The church is practically a breeding ground for power-seeking clergy.

Tradition supports the fact that preachers across denominational lines are worshipped and revered by the masses, especially in the African American community where I was born and raised. African Americans have a tremendous amount of respect and trust for the clergy. In all reality, this loyalty may have spun out of the civil-rights era whereby it was significantly imperative that those within the community rely on the merit of church leaders. Nevertheless, people today still go to great lengths to esteem their leaders, often exceeding safe and/or needful limits.

To some extent, the people must assume responsibility for the preacher's haughty and greedy spirits as they have built the mounting pedestals the preachers subsequently perch upon. In like manner, the preachers must acknowledge the fact that they have become absorbed, enchanted, and mesmerized by their own charm and finesse. As leaders, we are constantly being subjected to fame and notoriety, yet we cannot allow such occasions to lead us to self-inflation. We must constantly strive to keep arrogance and pride in check.

Aside from a pure lust for power itself, there is perhaps a logical reason why some preachers are so addicted to power's offspring. In my opinion, for some of these men and women, church was the first place they were ever really accepted. Basically they were revered as people of low esteem with inferior qualities and were perhaps even considered to be socially indigent. Yet they went to church, professed Jesus Christ, performed a few gifts, acknowledged a call to preach, and, *poof,* they were instantly crowned and merited as kings and queens. But instead of them humbling themselves before God and honoring him with their gifts and callings, they've become self-impressed, elated with the meaningless rewards their position and status has yielded—having lost themselves in the reverie of the "Holywood" image.

Groupie Love

> To the elders among you, I appeal as a fellow elder, a witness of Christ's suffering and one who also will share in the glory to be revealed: Be shepherds of God's flock that is under your care, serving as overseers—not because you must, but because you are willing, as God wants you to be; not greedy for money, but eager to serve; not lording it over those entrusted to you, but being an example to the flock. And when the Chief Shepherd appears, you will receive the crown of glory that will never fade away.
>
> 1 Peter 5.1-5 (NIV)

Before I go any farther, I'm inspired to stop and commend the shepherds and associates who care for the vigor of the flock. Not every preacher is guilty of abusing the sheep. I know that. However, what this chapter is emphasizing is vain glory and the abuse of power. You should know that anything practiced in extremes will ultimately end in ruin. Therefore we must do everything with godly discretion, being watchful, diligent in prayer, and on full-scale alert.

The enemy is crafty and full of deception, and preachers who overwhelmingly respond to the applause and the accolades of the people will in time become self imposed, believing themselves to be something they are not (Galatians 6:3). That's the spirit we want to avoid.

Unlike those who become self-impressed, spiritually mature preachers can differentiate between the compliments of the true supporters and the pseudo love of the groupies. However, discerning the genuine intent of the follower's heart may take a moment to process (remember Paul and the young fortune teller), but eventually God will reveal it to you. When he does, don't dismiss it. Women in general are excellent discerners. In fact, we are inherently sensitive, both naturally and spiritually. Yet we regularly dismiss intuitive "vibes" for fear of misjudging prematurely or perhaps appearing too critical. No doubt in some instances this statement bears accurate weight, not withstanding the fact that one should never substantiate presumable or assumptive evidence. However, once you've heeded the directives of the Holy Spirit, by all means, trust your God-given instincts. Chances are you're probably right.

Throughout your ministry you need to stop and assess the motives of the people who are pressing their way into your inner circle. Ask yourself, "Why are these people here? What do they really want from me? Am I secretly becoming addicted to their presence and applause?"

No matter the terrain, the scriptures tell us that people followed Jesus everywhere he went. His name was known throughout the region of Judea. Yet he was never captivated by their accolades. Jesus knew the same people crying, "Hosanna," on Monday, come Friday would be shouting, "We want Barabbas! Crucify him!"

Every miracle Jesus performed was indicative of his purpose. It was never to boost or build his reputation. He knew who he was and what he was called to do. Jesus was on a "God" mission, and he didn't let anything or anyone stop him. There will always be people who will try to join themselves to you and your aspired fame. As strange as it may seem, groupies assume if they are in the presence of greatness they too will be revered as great. Beloved, don't be swooned by the flattery of their lips; groupie love is extremely toxic. More often than not, groupies want to use you to get behind the curtains where they can mingle with the stars. If you allow lust to cause you to fall under their hypnotic trance, you'll eventually develop a false sense of glorification and superiority. Much like Lucifer, you too will be disgraced and ousted from your position.

I've said it before, and I'll say it again, you can't rely on people's temporal displays of affection as a sign of success. People change allegiance very quickly. My husband told me years ago, "Compliments are like perfume; you can smell it, but don't drink it!" Preachers,

I must warn you, don't let the people turn you into their celebrities. Paul immediately stopped the people at Lystra from trying to worship him and Barnabas. You too must correct people when they become overtly infatuated with your popularity, charisma, and status. God alone is to be worshipped, and he will not share his glory with another:

> When the crowd saw what Paul had done, they shouted in the Lycaonian language, "The gods have come down to us in human form!" Barnabas they called Zeus, and Paul they called Hermes because he was the chief speaker. The priest of Zeus, whose temple was just outside the city, brought bulls and wreaths to the city gates because he and the crowd wanted to offer sacrifices to them. But when the apostles Barnabas and Paul heard of this, they tore their clothes and rushed out into the crowd, shouting: "Men, why are you doing this? We too are only men, human like you. We are bringing you good news, telling you to turn from these worthless things to the living God, who made heaven and earth and sea and everything in them."
>
> Acts 14:11-15 (NIV)

For the Love of Money and Fame

> Here is a trustworthy saying: If anyone sets his heart on being an overseer [bishop], he desires a noble task. Now the overseer must be above

> reproach, the husband of but one wife, temperate,
> self-controlled, respectable, hospitable, able to
> teach, not given to drunkenness, not violent but
> gentle, not quarrelsome, not a lover of money.

1 Timothy 3:1-3 (NIV)

If power is the leading force behind the Holywood obsession, the love of money must be its proud and faithful ally. Charlatans (wolves in sheep's clothing) frequently prey on the soulful emotions and amiable resources of innocent church-going people. Sometimes these wolves are difficult to recognize because they come in such various disguises. But make no mistake about it; they're out there, lurking behind pulpits all over the country. However, for one to preach the gospel for any other reason than Luke 4:18-19, "to proclaim good news to the poor, declare spiritual freedom to the prisoner, healing of sight to the blind, deliverance for the oppressed, and God's favor to all mankind," is to overtly dishonor and insult God (NIV). What a shame! Consider the following scriptures:

> Now for some time a man named Simon had
> practiced sorcery in the city and amazed all
> the people of Samaria. He boasted that he was
> someone great, and all the people, both high and
> low, gave him their attention and exclaimed,
> "This man is the divine power known as the
> Great Power."

Acts 8:9-10 (NIV)

When Simon saw that the Spirit was given at the laying on of the apostles' hands, he offered them money and said, "Give me also this ability so that everyone on whom I lay my hands may receive the Holy Spirit." Peter answered, "May your money perish with you, because you thought you could buy the gift of God with money! You have no part or share in this ministry, because your heart is not right before God" (Acts 8:18-21, NIV).

Money and fame mustn't ever be your motivation for preaching the gospel. Contrary to popular opinion, you are a servant of God and not a hireling. How do you set a fair price on preaching, anyway? What is a reasonable figure? You must go wherever God sends you, regardless of the wages. I promised the Lord years ago that I would go wherever he sent me. I've literally preached in countries around the world, oftentimes for a little or nothing. Yet I went in obedience to the Lord's command. Perhaps we should place a mental marker at this juncture, as it is important for you to determine beforehand whether God sent you, or, for whatever reason, you sent yourself. Think about it; how many preachers do you know, given the option, would elect to choose a hundred-dollar purse over a thousand-dollar one?

After all has been said and done, Jesus has promised to pay whatever is right in spite of what people may say or do. Unfortunately, some pastors and preachers will deliberately attempt to take advantage of you and your ministry. Even so, my philosophy for preaching is simple: freely God has given, and freely I must give. Of course, I'm not by any means suggesting that taking advantage of a preacher is suitable; that would be completely absurd. Surely every believer knows "the elders who direct the affairs of the church well are worthy of double honor, especially those whose work is preaching and teaching" (1 Timothy 5:17-18, NIV). For the scripture says, "Do not muzzle the ox while it is treading out the grain," and "the worker deserves his wages" (1 Timothy 5:18). Truly I concur. In fact, I have absolutely no difference of opinion. However, if God tells us to go, we must go and not let money be the deciding factor.

A Final Word

The conclusion and implications of this chapter are clearly identified through this final summation and, lest I forget, my own personal observation. Assessing this note from an external position, it may seem my general impressions of ministry, money, and notoriety, are perhaps outdated in comparison. Nevertheless, they are worthy of careful consideration and contemplation.

For more than ten years, my husband and I ministered overseas. During that time, we watched the churches in America embrace many eccentric trends and fads. To our surprise, many popular preachers, ministries, and Christian vocalists were advertising promotional ventures with worldly, secular artists. Nevertheless, I question how a secular artist can promote a spiritual revival.

As a preacher of the gospel, I'm compelled to voice my displeasure with this merging. Perhaps we should consult the scriptures. Again, I must reiterate—is Jesus alone not enough? Has progress actually forced us to rely on worldly methods, guest appearances, and name dropping as a means of winning souls in the twenty-first century? Is this what the church in America is doing in order to reach this new and upcoming generation? Beloved, what has happened to the ancient landmarks? *Selah*.

> Do not be yoked together with unbelievers. For what do righteousness and wickedness have in common? Or what fellowship can light have with darkness? What harmony is there between Christ and Belial? What does a believer have in common with an unbeliever? What agreement is there between the temple of God and Idols? For we are the temple of the living God.
>
> 2 Corinthians 6:14-16 (NIV)

Review Precepts

1. At the inception of the early church, the apostles warned us of mammon's potentiality to incite and inflict personal and communal danger.

2. Today, church meetings and conferences have rapidly become the networking capital of Christendom. Saints would never believe what's really for sale and/or negotiation at some of these pretentious gatherings—all they see are the money changers and the trafficking of goods.

3. When we covet God's glory, desiring to be high and lifted up, we position ourselves for demonic possession.

4. People love to mingle with people of prominence. Therefore, leaders must curtail their appetites and emotions or they will lose themselves in the "Holywood" hype.

5. Make no mistake about it, not all pastors and presbytery preach because they want to see sinners converted. Some ministers preach because it pays the bills, or in some cases, simply offers them a handsome salary.

6. Preaching is merely a matter of semantics once preachers lose their spiritual fervor. Thus, ministry at that point is simple routine and ho hum.

7. Never let financial figures determine your willingness to preach the gospel of Jesus Christ.

Blind Leaders

> He replied, "Every plant that my heavenly father
> has not planted will be pulled up by the roots.
> Leave them; they are blind guides. If a blind man
> leads a blind man, both fall into a pit."
>
> Matthew 15:13 (NIV)

*A*mazingly, preachers will assume responsibility for the spiritual lives of others without obtaining appropriate training, licensing, or tutelage. In most states in the country, you can't even fish without a license, yet preachers regularly abuse their ministerial privileges by disregarding the spiritual principles of authoritarian leadership. Blind leadership is not optional or debatable. God will not anoint an individual who chooses to operate independent to his elected authority—period!

Irrelative to one's gift, title, or position, everyone in ministry must be accountable to the recognized authorities of the church (if for no other reason than for guidance, support, and overall protection). Thus, the governing systems of the church should provide safety to the general populace—that subject alone would consume the contents of this chapter.

Collectively, the problem is much worse than any
of us can imagine. As it were, blind leaders frequently
migrate in and out of churches, making themselves
completely invisible and difficult to track. There are
blind leaders, and then, there are blind leaders —serial
leaders who boldly refuse to submit themselves to
anyone, let alone the spiritual authority of the church.
Reasoning with these individuals is impossible. As far
as they are concerned, they are their own authority—
self-ruled! Contrary to what they may think or believe,
they've been deceived by the forces of darkness. They
say, "Man didn't call me to preach. God did. Therefore,
I don't answer to man, I only answer to God." To
God! What god? What god endorses rebellion and
insubordination? Beloved, this philosophy is not in any
shape supported by the Holy scriptures.

I've taken the time to expound on this point because
blind leadership is a serious infraction against the Lord
and his church. Heretofore, I cannot reiterate this
mandate enough. God will not promote, support, or
endorse a man or a minister who will not submit him
or herself to his elected authority. When preachers act
out behaving in a rebellious fashion, only to say, "This
is of God," it opens the door to demonic infestation. By
and large, blind leaders are a menace to the Christian
church. In fact, they lead many shallow believers down
paths of total destruction, and they aren't in the least bit
concerned with the health, safety, or spiritual growth of
the sheep.

Thus, blind leaders deceive and manipulate people
by binding them to the "*isms* of men." Such are

traditionalism, legalism, and denominationalism. These men and women interject fear and control over the people by demonstrating the following behaviors: pseudo or false gifts, stringent authority and abuse of power, scriptural distortion, and preaching what they call a "revolutionary-never-before-heard-of gospel." This is exactly how many cults are formed. In fact, it is the actual blueprint for spiritual error and deception.

Concerned? You should be. Perhaps the next time Willie and Wilma Wonka hand you their impressive resume, you'll stop and ask yourself these important questions: "Is this individual submitted to a legitimate authority? How do I know if he or she is a wolf is sheep's clothing—a blind leader?" Well, first and foremost, the Bible says, "A tree is recognized by his fruit" (Matthew 12:33, NIV). Since fruit doesn't grow over night, it may take you some time to get to know them (Matthew 12:33, NIV). In addition, other symptoms will limpidly reveal their essence as well:

- They deny the deity of Christ and the Apostolic Creed.
- They prohibit the true (authentic) move of God.
- They demonstrate a form of godliness but deny the power thereof.
- They desire to build a self-made monument to their own accomplished achievements—not to the expansion of the Lord's church.
- They don't walk in love.

- They frequently consume the spotlight by directing others toward themselves.

- They are un-teachable and un-reachable.

- They discourage empowerment amongst the people by encouraging them to become dependant upon them and their teaching.

- They frequently operate in one or more of the following spirits: manipulation, control, and/ or witchcraft.

- They prey on weak-willed, silly men and women who are gullible, zealous for attention, and long to be accepted and esteemed.

In conjunction to their many foul acts of indiscretion, blind leaders are perhaps most dangerous because they are usually gifted, intelligent, and extremely charismatic. These traits alone afford them ample accessibility, visibility, and attention from within the congregation. Blind leaders want people to believe they are immutable, and their word is "the word of the Lord," no questions asked. Nevertheless, if saints would get in the book and discover their place and position of spiritual authority, blind leaders would lose their potency. Bottom line: if we the church, the ecclesia of Christ, refuse to follow their leadership. They'd eventually stop trying to lead. In fact, we'd run them clean out of business. The problems we're seeing in our churches today are a direct result of blind leadership and, yes, misinformed saints.

The Church: Every Member Counts

Did you not know every member in the body of Christ matters? Again, Paul described the church as a body, an ingeniously designed system that operates dependent on the inter workings of each intrinsic part. Simply put, every born-again believer is essential to the building of the body of Christ. The church (all encompassing) embodies millions and millions of people, all of whom are inherently gifted to operate simultaneously as one unified force with one goal-oriented purpose and one amiable cause. In contrast, many of our churches today are broken and fragmented as leaders are "doing their own thing" and are totally overlooking the primary purpose for the church's existence.

While our demonstration of worship may greatly differ, the essence of our faith should remain synonymous. As it were, we are joined in celebration by an insurmountable host of witnesses, both in heaven and on earth. Even Christ himself "sits at the right hand of the Father as He makes intercession for us" (Romans 8:34, NIV). According to Ephesians 4:8, "When he ascended on high he lead captivity captive, and gave gifts unto men." Therefore, the Holy Spirit has enabled each member of the body of Christ with the grace and spiritual fortitude to build, edify, and encourage one's self as he or she endeavors to encourage others.

Embracing/Understanding Full Body Ministry

Paul said there were a multitude of callings and demonstrations of the Spirit. Moreover, as the church grows into its perfected (mature) form, it will eventually operate and function as the Lord designed—fully equipped to do the work of the ministry. Spiritual maturity should in fact empower and propel believers to go and grow beyond salvation—onward, toward intrepid discipleship. I call this New Testament concept full-body ministry.

In the past, the church has primarily disregarded the fundamental principles of full-body ministry by encircling itself around a few select ministers, churches, gifts, methods, and/or denominations. As a result, spiritual growth has been severely stunted—producing (in part) a powerless church. Case in point: years ago, the ministry gift of the prophet and the apostle were basically unheard of. In fact, many pastors didn't even believe the two offices were viable, let alone *necessary* in today's ministry. As a result, they were blatantly pushed out of the inner circle, and the church was denied access and exposure to their ministry gifts. Many of the pastors who shunned the two offices did so for one or more of the following reasons:

1. Spiritual ignorance and misconceptions.
2. Totally "brain washed" by the philosophies and traditions of men.
3. A previous series of unfortunate events.

As leaders in the body of Christ, we can usher spiritual maturity into the house of God if we are willing to dismiss our prejudice and heed to the moving of the Holy Spirit. In order to maximize discipleship, fortitude, and spiritual agility, we must release the spiritual gifts to flow fluently throughout the body of Christ.

However, it is imperative that we do not confuse emotionalism with the spiritual manifestations of the Holy Spirit nor impede divine order and/or tolerate irreverent misconduct. All things must be done decently and in order. Of course, that should go without saying. Nevertheless, if we fail to utilize all the gifts Christ gave the early church, we are going to be weak, malnourished, and ill-equipped to fight in these latter times.

There are many gifts and callings we have yet to see manifested in our meetings. However, fear has chased many pastors behind the walls of safety and seclusion, as some leaders have attempted to control the demonstration of the spirit by mastering the use of ritualistic methods, humanistic systems, and organized religion. Yet with all due respect, it is time for the church to be the church (singular). We must lay aside foolish arguments and seek the Lord for understanding and revelation. If we don't, the church will never reach its maximum height of spiritual maturity—at least not right away.

I'm fully persuaded that the church needs everything the Lord left behind: the five-fold ministry gifts (the apostle, prophet, evangelist, pastor, and teacher), the nine manifestations of the spirit (prophecy, tongues, interpretations of tongues, gifts of healings, faith, miracles, words of wisdom, knowledge, and discerning of spirits), and all the other ministerial gifts of helps and support (exhortation, governments, giving, intercession, mercy, administration, teaching, etcetera). Paul said, "We should eagerly desire spiritual gifts as all of these must be done for the strengthening of the church" (1 Corinthians 14:26, NIV). For confirmation, read all of 1 Corinthians 14.

Beloved, spiritual growth and development is continually evolving (Hebrews 6:1-2, NIV). Every day, we must add to our faith by working out our own salvation with fear and trembling (Philippians 2:12). If we want our roots to go deeper in Christ, we must cultivate the ground on a daily basis, preparing it for spiritual increase and the anticipatory endowment of supernatural power. If leaders aspire to raise healthy, balanced, and viable sheep, they need to ensure their members receive the following: exposure to the five-fold ministry gifts, prayer support via intercession, and *dunamis* demonstrations of the Holy Spirit (*dunamis* being the Greek word for power, might, work, deed, or ability).

Diverting Discrimination and Class Systems

During the Cold War era, many socialist societies embraced the Marxist teachings of the class system.

Several years ago, Hurricane Katrina shocked Americans as she left behind a vivid illustration of what the formal system may have resembled. There were no gray areas, just a patent description of "those who had and those who had not."

For centuries, the church has been divided over everything from racial equality and baptismal methods to speaking in tongues and the laying on of hands. Yet, in so doing, blind leaders have interfered with the natural mitosis and development of maturing sheep by confusing them over unnecessary rudiments that bind them to the law.

Paul warned the believers at Galatia about the dangers of mixing salvation with legalism. Pastors do not have to shepherd sick diseased sheep. However, blind leaders can't steer blind followers. Preachers and pastors must create a loving, spirit-filled environment whereby they and their sheep can grow and develop.

A healthy spirit-lead environment will emphatically shun all forms of discrimination. God confronted Peter's racial biases in a vision of unclean beasts. (Refer to Acts 10 and pay especially close attention to verses 28, 34, and 35 NIV). He said to them, "You are well aware that it is against the law for a Jew to associate with a Gentile or visit him. But God has shown me that I should not call any man impure or unclean" (NIV). Verses thirty-four and thirty-five say, "Then Peter began to speak, 'I now realize how true it is that God does not show favoritism but accepts men from every nation who fear him and do what is right.'"

Equality should not only be heralded in words but demonstrated in one's acts and deeds. Moreover, every man, woman, boy, and girl is important to God and deserves mutual respect. Regardless of one's economic status, nationality, educational background, sexual preference, or political persuasion, we all need salvation. Therefore, if discrimination of any kind is embraced among the leadership, it will eventually infect the attitude of the flock.

How well does your congregation receive people from other races and ethnicities? How do the people in your church treat one another? Well, consider this hometown example: years ago, my husband would carry van loads of homeless people to church with us every Sunday evening. As a rule, the ushers would automatically seat us in the rear section, to the left, toward the exits. The congregation in concert (it seemed) would look behind them to watch the transients file into the building. As we approached the point in the service when the pastor invited everyone to get out of their seats and welcome their neighbors, the homeless people were reserved to hugging each other as the congregation was not very eager to mingle with them. The looks on their faces soberly revealed their desire to be touched and loved. Yet they smelled, and they knew they smelled. Nevertheless, a few of us would hold our breath and hug as many as we could. In actuality, it really didn't matter how bad they smelled. God loved them, and it was important to us that we show them the same extent of kindness we'd show anyone else in the church. Now, if you'd have asked some of the other people in the congregation if their failure to connect with the homeless people was a sign of bias and discrimination, they all would have emphatically denied it. Nevertheless, their attitude and expressions clearly confirmed their position.

Beloved, we should not take issues of diversity lightly, as it is an important principle in kingdom living. This is the conclusion of the matter: the face of God is not a color or pigmentation, ethnicity or origin, it's simply love. 1 Corinthians 13:1-3 says it all:

> And now I will show you the most excellent way. If I speak in the tongues of men and angels, but have not love, I am only a resounding gong or a clanging cymbal. If I have the gift of prophecy and can fathom all mysteries and all knowledge, and if I have a faith that can move mountains, but have not love, I am nothing. If I give all I possess to the poor and surrender my body to the flames, but have not love, I gain nothing.
>
> (NIV)

For your own personal study on discrimination, favoritism, and diversity, refer to James 2 and 3.

Understanding Diversity in the Church Today

A global-minded leader has the ability to reach people from different cultures and nationalities. They are preachers with a vision that spans beyond their own race and people. Incidentally, the church is not black or white, though we often visualize it as such. Nonetheless, it is made up of a rainbow of people from various nations, cultures and ethnicities.

People everywhere share the same basic needs: food, shelter, belonging, and acceptance. Yet I have lived as an American abroad in both Asia and Europe, and I can tell you getting acclimated to the customs and traditions of a foreign country is not easy. Americans who've had the privilege of living outside of the United States know all to well the importance of adjusting to the customs of a given society. The old cliché "When in Rome, do as the Romans do" is relatively true. Beloved, the same is also true of ministry. Paul said, "I have become all things to all men so that by all possible means I might save some" (1 Corinthians 9:22, NIV). There are those living right next door to you who perhaps look similar to you in appearance but are foreigners to your faith, completely unaware of the ideals and beliefs you practice and share. Yet ministering to them is not difficult if you understand where they're coming from. Consequently, the only way to find out is to take the time to get to know them. "The fruit of the righteous is a tree of life, and he who wins souls is wise" (Proverbs 11:30, NIV).

There is a vital link between success and ministry, and that link is called *understanding*. Solomon, the world's wisest man, said in Proverbs 4:7, "Wisdom is supreme; therefore get wisdom. Though it costs all you have, get understanding" (NIV). I like the way it reads in the King James Version: "Wisdom is the principle thing; therefore get wisdom: and with all thy getting get an understanding."

On the grand scale of ministry, pulpit preaching only consumes a minor percentage of your time and energy (Moses's father-in-law tried to warn him of that very reality). So whether it is counseling or fellowship, most lay preachers spend the bulk of their time directly ministering to others. So what does it mean to minister to the body of Christ? In laymen's terms, it means having the spiritual knowledge, skills, and ability to interact with others at a level by which they can relate and understand, prayerfully provoking constructive change and/or transformation.

Looking beyond this definition, let's go back to the topic of diversity. Overall, ministry in and of itself can be difficult, and the diversity factor makes that interaction even harder. But let's face it; the shades of ministry are changing. People don't want to be a part of a racially or denominationally biased church. They want to be a part of a ministry that not only offers them spiritual growth and increase, but can also relate to their cultural differences as well.

In order to effectively minister to those outside of your race and ethnicity (especially in the areas of counseling), you'll need to gather cultural information. In general, people simply behave in response to their customs and cultural upbringing. If you understand that in advance, it will be much easier for you to interact with them.

In the spring of 2004, I was invited to speak at this little rustic church in Kaiserslautern, Germany.

Unfortunately I didn't know wine was such a valued commodity among the Europeans. Well, I soon found out. After the message, the pastor gave me an expensive bottle of German wine—a complimentary gift. At first I was completely shocked. Then I became a little offended, but after a few minutes I soon realized the people were not trying to be rude or unspiritual; they were simply acting within their custom. In their eyes, the wine was an honorable gift, so I gladly received it and used it to make a lovely marinade for my Christmas duck.

All in all, there are many barriers that obstruct communication and exchange: racial barriers, social barriers, cultural barriers, spiritual barriers, and psychological barriers. However, you can't please everybody—that is the first rule of thumb. In any given situation, having followed the rules of diversity and carefully assessed the contents of the complaint, someone is going to be unhappy with the decision you make. That's life. Perhaps with a little grace you can win a few good-will points for being a good listener, but other than that, you can't take it personally.

Our spiritual children are very similar to our biological children. They have their own personality, temperament, and traits. Yet as parents, we must learn how to minister to each of them on a personal level without making comparisons, initiating competition, or expressing acts of favoritism. No doubt we all have children—both natural and spiritual, who make us proud, get on our nerves, keeps us laughing, or cause us great sorrow. However, we love them all and make every attempt to avoid marked displays of affection and preferential treatment.

Note: Churches who service a multicultural congregation should formulate diversity programs where leadership can learn how to minister to people from other races, backgrounds, and cultures. Actually, every church with a vision for diversity should do this. You will discover the training you receive will enable you to expand your scope of possibilities by bettering your counseling and administrative skills.

The Dos and Don'ts of Counseling

Leaders are expected to give sound counsel. Quite commonly, people assume because you are a preacher that they can safely confide in you for wisdom and advice. After all, a preacher is supposed to have "spiritual insight." Right? Right! The Bible teaches us there is safety in a multitude of counsel. Therefore, it is strongly recommended you surround yourself with an ample circle of trusted leaders. I must inform you, it is not a sign of ignorance or weakness to ask someone for assistance. In fact, nobody in their right mind would assume that your inquiry is due to a lack of spirituality. If you ask me, it's wisdom. Personally, I don't want to be responsible for misleading or misdirecting God's people. Therefore I carefully assess what I say to parishioners. I also scrutinize, reiterate, and clearly differentiate what I have said from what God has said. Saints, beware of people who always "have a word for you from the Lord." In addition, you too must also be very careful. When you tell people God said something, you better know he said it. If not, you'll mislead people, causing them to fall to error.

Where Do I Begin?

Before I begin any counseling session, I usually ask myself two specific questions: "What does the parishioner want from me?" and "Am I able to give them what they need?" If I'm not completely satisfied with either answer, I will boldly recommend them to someone who can help them. Moreover, time is of the essence, both theirs and mine, and I don't want to spend weeks or perhaps even months wandering around the same tree. So if after the first few sessions I find I'm not effective, I will graciously release them to seek other counsel.

Occasionally you will be faced with situations that are above your level of knowledge and expertise. However, if you want to eliminate confusion and misunderstanding, you need to consult the wisdom of your leadership. They are your safety net. Issues such as child abuse, homicide, and suicide should automatically be reported to the leadership as well as to the proper authorities. At all costs, you want to avoid the fault or risk of overlooking or underrating a potentially life-threatening situation. Practice asking open ended questions—not closed, "yes or no" questions. For example, you wouldn't ask the parishioner, "Are you sad?" That would require a yes or no answer. Instead, you would ask, "What's causing you to feel sad?" or "Why are you sad?"

Again, accountability and homework are forthcoming. Beloved, you want to know ahead of time what you are getting yourself into. Preachers, male and female, should carefully consider all precautionary measures prior to accepting a case. For one, you need to support the wingman concept by exercising the buddy system (don't get caught alone with a crazed individual). Two, you need to establish the client's purpose for soliciting your assistance. You can accomplish this by asking several open ended questions. And thirdly, you need to trust your natural instincts (if it doesn't feel right, back out gracefully). The woman-in-distress syndrome has brought many pastors and preachers (especially males) to ruin. Teamwork is absolutely essential.

Of all the internal systems functioning within the Christian church today, checks and balances remains underutilized. If pastors and preachers were unified within their communities, cities, and states, churches would not be vandalized by blind leaders who are unmarked and unsuspected. Paul frequently warned the Christian churches of the dangers of wolves—those who masquerade as angels of light. With lawsuits and other litigation on a steady rise, we must be diligent, coherent, and concerned for the welfare of our fellow man.

The Danger of Cliques

Now, concerning cliques: cliques are formed when people of similar personalities bond together. Naturally people are more comfortable with people who share the same common interests, and though these relationships may or may not pose a danger to the ministry itself, if barriers of any kind restrict others from feeling welcome, it is indeed a potential problem. I have actually known sects or groups who've controlled admission to their church circles on the basis of others not "fitting their image."

Clergy should vehemently discourage such behavior. Overall, cliques are a multi-faceted problem that affects every known system in the civilized world, both formal and informal. Whether it is a church member, fraternity, sorority, street gang, or country club, it's all the same. It is my experience the bigger, more popular, or more gifted the church or organization, the more possibilities for compartmentalized cliques to develop. There are several reasons why this theory is plausible:

1. People become lifted up in pride. "My pastor, church, choir, etcetera, is better than yours."

2. People become self-righteous. "Because we have the grandest teaching, spiritual demonstrations, and worship, we are more spiritual."

3. People become selfish. "This is our church, our pastor and our music department, and we don't want to share it with anybody else."

Preachers, as much as lies within you, you must remain inclusive. Your pastors and leaders need you to be open and versatile, able to promote and emulate God's love to everyone that comes within your church doors. This is especially important for mega churches where senior leadership is unable to physically touch everyone. You are their tentacles. Without you, people will get lost in the massive crowds. Soon after, they will begin to foster feelings of insignificance and, eventually, disappear.

Stuffy, stoic churches release an air of superiority and self-inflation that often deters visitors and potential members. So I offer a word to the wise: advertising is indeed an effective tool for recruiting membership, but word of mouth always produces the best results. Every now and then, you need to stop and consider your church's atmosphere, climate, and communal reputation because time does bring about changes. Think about it: how would you feel if you were the visitor in your church?

Hypocrisy in the Church

How can you say to your brother, "Brother, let me take the speck out of your eye," when you yourself fail to see the plank in your own eye? You hypocrites first take the plank out of your eye, and then you will see clearly to remove the speck from your brother's eye.

Luke 6:42 (NIV)

Although I briefly alluded to hypocrisy and realism in "Pulpit Etiquette," the subject is worth further discussion, especially since blind leaders specialize in the art of hypocrisy. I personally can't stress enough the importance of realism. Many of us who grew up in the church twenty or thirty years ago saw so much hypocrisy, it's a miracle we still want anything to do with institutionalized religion. Fortunately, our love for God, his people, and the Christian church serve as the binding tie that seals our loyalty. Yet in spite of what we saw growing up as children and adolescents, most of us knew it was not the example Christ wanted the church to present.

Jesus hated the antics of the hypocritical Pharisees, calling them empty sepulchers, stumbling blocks, and blind leaders (Matthew 23:27-28).

Incidentally, sinners around the globe speculatively know how church people are supposed to act. In fact, Hollywood regularly ridicules us in sitcoms and comedy shows, and we foolishly join in the hee-haw. Saints, it all boils down to this: the church is afraid to honestly admit we are human. In fact, we are just as vulnerable as any other person to the lusts of the flesh. Instead of us being ourselves by admitting that we too were once sinners saved by grace, we pretend to be something we are not, and when we are caught in the folly of our ways, we're labeled as narrow minded and hypocritical.

I wonder if we are the real reason people don't want to go to church anymore. Have we disgraced Christ by our behavior and conduct? Jerry Adler in his *Newsweek* article entitled "Spirituality in America" contended that Christianity is still the primary religion of choice, but, in general, people do not attend conventional church meetings like they used to. Although the world wants a taste of spirituality and religion, they don't want the Jesus of the Bible. While that in many ways is due to the image we have presented, Ezekiel 36:23 says, "I will show the holiness of my name, which has been profaned among the nations" (NIV). The King James Version uses the word *heathen*. Saints, regardless of our pleas, sermons, CDs, DVDs, or movies, we cannot deny the fact that the world is watching us and judging the Christ we preach about by the conduct we present. If we look, act, and behave like unchanged men, the world will honestly view and conclude that that's exactly who and what we are. Refer to Matthew 23:12-34.

Denominational Superiority Complex

> All things have I seen in the days of my vanity: there is a just man that perisheth, in his righteousness, and there is a wicked man that prolongeth his life in his wickedness. Be not righteous over much, neither make thyself over wise: why shouldesth, thou destroy thyself? Be not over much wicked, neither be though foolish: why shouldesth thou die before thy time? It is good that thou shouldest take hold of these (balance); yea, also from this withdraw not thine hand: for he that feareth God shall come forth of them all.
>
> Ecclesiastes 7:15-18 (KJV)

Leaders are sometimes blinded by the notion their church and denomination is better than everyone else's. They spend valuable time arguing and debating denominational issues instead of preaching the word of God. Beloved, when your denominational convictions are overemphasized, institutionalized converts and potential clones are produced. An institutionalized convert builds his or her faith on the doctrines of men instead of on the principles of Christ. Paul asked the church at Galatia this question: "You foolish Galatians! Who has bewitched you? Before your very eyes Jesus Christ was clearly portrayed as crucified, I would like to learn just one thing from you: Did you receive the Spirit by observing the law, or by believing what you heard? Are you so foolish? After beginning with the Spirit, are you now trying to attain your goal by human effort?" (Galatians 3:1-3, NIV).

One thing is certain. Your doctrine doesn't save; Jesus saves. Though you may possess some very strong convictions, they alone cannot convert or transform a life. Those who try to live by the law will eventually die by the law. It's all about God's unmerited favor. "For it is by grace you have been saved through faith—and this is not from yourselves, it is the gift of God—not by works so that no one can boast" (Ephesians 2:8-9, NIV).

Lady preacher, teach people how to access heaven for the help they need (not you or your church's tenets). Otherwise they will become disenchanted and turn to worldly practitioners, doctrines of demons, and godless fetishes for the answers they seek. Such practices are manifested in the form of rabbit's feet, charms, beads, bones, crystals, dead saints, horoscopes, numerology, water witching, self-god theology, new-age philosophy, gold dust, ancient mythology, paganism, repetitious prayers, mind over matter, and/or any one or more of the many other manmade litanies available today. Beloved, these things are absolutely futile—lifeless and ineffective. The rudimentary systems of men are powerless against the forces of darkness:

> It is for freedom that Christ has set you free. Stand firm, then, and do not let yourselves be burdened again by a yoke of slavery. Mark my words! I, Paul, tell you if you let yourselves be circumcised, Christ will be of no value to you at all. Again I declare to every man who lets himself be circumcised that he is obligated to obey the whole law. You who are trying to be justified by law have been alienated from Christ; you have fallen away from grace. But by faith we eagerly await through the Spirit of righteousness for which we hope. For in Christ Jesus neither circumcision nor uncircumcised has any value. The only thing that counts is faith expressing itself through love.
>
> Galatians 5:1-6 (NIV)

Furthermore, when preachers coerce people into abiding by their own personal convictions, denominational regulations (not the word of God), old wives' tales, and the traditions of men, they are binding them to religion, and religion is about rudiments and rituals—not relationship. Anyone who promotes and elevates their denomination above everyone else's simply does not understand the concept of body ministry.

I will close with this: one day I was talking to a pastor friend of mine, and I asked her why she thought the church was not flowing in miracles today like they were in biblical days, and she said something I thought was very profound:

> God is holding back the signs and wonders until the church—the apostles, prophets, evangelist, pastors, and teachers (the five-fold ministry)— starts moving as one body. The attention cannot be directed toward one or two men. It has to be the unified body of Christ moving as one.
>
> Barbara Bellamy (2007)

Review Precepts

1. When ministers abuse their ministerial privileges in order to pursue their personal agendas, people are wounded and broken in the wake.

2. Church leaders must debunk blind leaders, not only for the sake of the ministry, but for the health of the general populace as well.

3. Blind leaders can only do what we the people, the church, allow them to do. Bottom line: if we'd stop following their leadership, they'd have no one to govern.

4. Blind leaders and covert sins are a well-kept secret in some Christian circles. The cover up is similar in part to the internal workings of a secret society.

5. The church today needs rousting, as she is under the hypnotic trance of charismatic leaders whose objectives are to build sand castles in the sky.

Fallen Angels

*H*elp! I've fallen and I can't get up! In October 1990, Life-Call Personal Emergency Response Systems awakened the nation with this alarming slogan. Suddenly people were expressing sympathy for those who'd fallen and couldn't get back up. In a very similar way, spiritual incidents of falling also induce compassion and sympathetic awareness. Regardless of church affiliation or tenure of Christian experience, anybody anywhere is capable of falling. And if the notion of falling isn't bad enough, the idea of falling beyond one's ability to rescue oneself is even more disturbing. But how does a born again, blood-bought believer fall from grace? What happens? Are there no warning signs? No escape hatches?

There are actually two specific reasons why Christians fall. The first reason is found in James 1:13-15: "When tempted, no one should say, God is tempting me. For God cannot be tempted by evil, nor does he tempt anyone; but each one is tempted when, by his own evil desire, he is dragged away and enticed. Then, after desire has conceived, it gives birth to sin; and sin, when it is full-grown, gives birth to death" (NIV).

For years, Satan has thoroughly studied you—your ancestral history, relational history, even your environmental history, and he knows all too well the weakened, fragmented, and fractured areas in your life. In fact, he uses those (exact) human insults to endanger and permanently entrap you.

It is not difficult to ascertain how from the core of that very consciousness the sins of the father emerge. Thus, the ghastly plan of the enemy is aided by Satan's vicious plot to arrest your conscience and impound your will, even to the extent of curtailing your earnest desire to conquer and defeat secret struggles. The battle is real, and the fight is on!

By and large, Satan is on the prowl, and if the truth be told, he's wasting no time selecting victims. In fact, the sooner he can destroy and corrupt your moral innocence, the better. That deceitful jackal will prey on every vulnerability (those known and unknown to you). Whether mental, emotional, physical, sexual, or social—it doesn't really matter—Satan's after blood. Like Peter, Lucifer desires to sift you as wheat. *Sift* in this context means "get rid of or something unwanted." Satan wants to get rid of you by making you an ineffective agent for the Lord. And he has the skills to do it. If Satan can cause you to stumble and fall, he can contaminate your witness and weaken your testimony. His objective is to swing the carrot of temptation before you like the steady motion of a pendulum, back and forth, over and over, until you either cling to God and resist his advances or succumb to temptation, regress, and fall.

Beloved, Satan knows that if you're lacking in faith, fellowship, or prayer, you won't have the power to resist his seduction. Therefore, it is only a matter of time before you accept his vile invitation and find yourself falling from grace.

Fallen Heroes

In 1987, the church suffered a debilitating blow when Pastor Jim Bakker, the CEO of the PTL Club, and Evangelist Jimmy Swaggart publicly confessed their incidents of falling. These two great men suffered irrefutable damage to both their character and ministries as a result of their indiscretions. They were men of God, secretly engulfed in a private world of sin, and nobody knew they were falling. As painful as it was, the evangelists' confessions momentarily awakened the Christian church. Many pastors and preachers who were secretly involved in sin were instantly delivered, or perhaps scared straight, because God was exposing the works of darkness, and they feared the possibility of public exposure.

According to modern-day psychologists, when a significant incident or event occurs, specific imprints of the experience are permanently registered in the memory of one's mind. The impression is so pronounced, one can recall exactly where and what they were doing at the apex of that moment. Well, like millions of other American's that day, I too was sitting in front of the television set, gazing at the preacher's broken countenance. Back then, I was a young, naïve believer, yet I was addicted to Evangelist Swaggart's ministry. Undoubtedly, he was by far my favorite TV preacher, and because of my personal affection for his ministry, I blamed the saints for their lack of compassion and stone-wall response to his poignant confession. I remember questioning God, asking him again and again, "Lord, does anybody out there care about what he is going through? Where is everybody now? Can't they see he is hurting? Lord, how could you let this happen?" I cried and cried. I'd never seen a man of God fall in such anguish and disgrace.

Like many others in the body of Christ, I fell on my face and answered the call to prayer. Back then, I knew absolutely nothing about the power of intercession, yet that's exactly what God was calling me to do. Although I hadn't perfected the gift, with sorrow and lamentation I did what I knew how to do, and that was to cry out to the Lord until the burden lifted. All in all, my heart was heavy. I was sad for the preachers, sad for their families and followers, and sad for the church. Nevertheless, in the midst of it all, God showed me something I will never forget:

1. Never idolize flesh! This may seem strange, but I told you earlier that I had become very fond of Jimmy Swaggart's ministry. So much so I had begun to look at Brother Jimmy as a means of identifying with the works of Christ. Instead of looking at Jesus, who was actively operating in and through Brother Jimmy's ministry, I was

actually looking at flesh (man). The best way I know how to explain it is to say that I was praising God for what he was doing, but I was reverencing Jimmy Swaggart.

2. God loved Evangelists Bakker and Swaggart in spite of their offenses.

3. God always has compassionate, mature leaders who will humbly support and hold up the arms of the fallen.

4. Though it may look bleak today, the sun will come up tomorrow.

5. Church people are not always kind.

6. But for the grace of God, go I.

Perhaps the saddest commentary of all was the world's response to the evangelists' confessions. The general public had no idea how important it was for these fallen leaders to openly repent. They did not, nor could not, have understood the spiritual implications. All they wanted was a show. You see, pointing a finger at a fallen Christian leader temporarily enabled them to crudely condone their own attraction to sin.

Well beyond the church's control, the world laughed and ridiculed the fallen preachers. At every turn comedians, politicians, and even unwitting preachers mocked and ousted their disrepute. In reality, the tragic remains equated to this chilling fact: the world was not only laughing at Evangelists Bakker and Swaggart, they were laughing at the church and the entire body of Christ. Beloved, no man is an island, and no one is above the law of God—not the bishop, the cardinal, the apostle, the deacon, the musician, the janitor, or the usher. Need I say more? What's done in the dark will come to the light. Thus, every action whether good or bad, right or wrong, demands a candid response.

As Christians, we must purpose in our hearts to maintain holiness, not only for the sake of our own reputation, but for the sake of the church's, as well. Therefore, if we secretly hide our sins, we will eventually be put to shame. Refer to the story of King David, the Prophet Nathan, and David's wife, Bathsheba. It is found in 2 Samuel 12.

What Does It Mean to Fall?

> For though a righteous man falls seven times,
> he rises again, but the wicked are brought down
> by calamity.
>
> Proverbs 24:16 (NIV)

Webster defines *falling* in several different ways: "to descend freely from the force of gravity, to lower or to become lowered, to leave an erect position suddenly and involuntarily, or to commit an immoral act."

Have you ever fallen? Not necessarily from grace—just fallen. How did it make you feel? About twenty years ago, I was late picking up a friend from the Dallas-Fort Worth International Airport. As you can imagine, there was no available parking near the main gate, so I was forced to park about a seven-minute walk from the terminal (at least, that's what the sign said). I figured if they'd calculated the distance to be about seven minutes walking, a brisk sprint would get me there in about three minutes.

Somehow, while completely in motion, I tripped and fell head over foot in the middle of the parking lot. It was absolutely spontaneous. Like a stunt right out of Barnum and Bailey's circus, I rolled over like a cat on a hot tin roof. In fact, if you hadn't known any better, you'd thought I'd actually planned it. Though I was completely stunned, my greatest concern was not whether I was hurt, nor if I'd torn my favorite denim skirt, all I wanted to know was, "Who saw me fall?"

I quickly jumped up, dusted myself off, looked around the parking lot for spectators, and took off again. You see, I assumed because I didn't see anyone no one saw me. So what did I do? I got up and kept on running. I wanted to get out of the vicinity before I was caught and identified. But let's assume someone had seen me fall. Would I have reacted any differently? Perhaps I would have, especially if I'd known others knew about the falling.

Beloved, there's no doubt about it; exposure will definitely affect your attitude toward covert (hidden) sins. In fact, exposure will slap the arrogance right out of your defense. There are many reasons why getting caught will change your response to incidence of falling. Nevertheless, the effects of falling are (in all reality) relative to the will of the violator. For instance:

1. First and foremost, you must understand that some folks have no remorse; they're just sad they got caught. People who can openly confess Jesus Christ and comfortably walk in sin are blatantly deceiving themselves.

2. Getting caught means acknowledging your error. For some folks, as long as nobody knows, nobody takes responsibility for the action. This in turn suggests that many offenders, if not caught or convicted in their hearts to repent, will continue to walk in sin.

3. People who get caught either love or hate to be treated with "sympathetic awareness." Sympathetic awareness is any kind of expression of pity—positive or negative.

4. There is a tendency for the fallen to become defensive and angry with those who are laughing and snickering. I'm sorry, but frankly speaking, that's the price you pay for sin. Every time you miss the mark, somebody will be there to celebrate it. It's sad to say, but not everyone is *for* you. Some people are simply going to enjoy watching you suffer.

5. After the initial shock and shame, pride usually sets in. Some fallen foes tend to act un-phased by the unwelcome attention, when in reality they are plagued with guilt, condemnation, and thoughts of failure.

Very similar to my former example, some Christians tend to think if they don't get caught (or if they don't see eyes staring back at them), they are in the clear—free to disobey God without consequence or repercussion. But the Bible says, "Be not deceived; God is not mocked: for whatsoever a man soweth, that shall he also reap" (Galatians 6:7, KJV).

Remember, saints, God is watching, and to be honest about it, the world is watching too. In case you've forgotten, a minister of the gospel is forever under the watchful eye of the public. People constantly scrutinize your character and ministry for evidence of indiscretion. Criticism and defamation of character are common for those in the public eye. Whether the allegations against you are true or false, you'll never be able to elude rumors. One thing is certain; if you expect to survive in ministry, there are several things you have got to learn how to do:

1. Walk in forgiveness (shake it off).
2. Put off offense (guard your heart).
3. Develop a tough hide (what does it matter anyway?).
4. Foster a relentless spirit (stay on course).

Just the same, Jesus understood the sting of verbal assault. The world called him many evil things—even a devil. Nevertheless, Jesus said, "The God of this world has no place in me." My friend, accusations will come and accusations will go, but like Gamaliel told the men of the Sanhedrin Council when they blasphemed the Acts of the Apostles, "If these men's activities are from man they will fail; but if it is from God, you won't be able to stop them; you'll only find yourself fighting against God" (Acts 5:38-39, NIV).

You Don't Have to Fall

At one time, church leaders debated the scriptural accuracy of Pastor Donnie McClurkin's hit single "We Fall Down." Though some found discrepancies with the song's theology, many people were emphatically supportive. I understand. The possibility of inherently possessing the gene that predisposes you to falling undoubtedly disturbs some people. Nevertheless, Paul recognized the vulnerability of the flesh and encouraged believers on every occasion to avoid the wistful ambitions of the flesh by staying connected to him—Jesus Christ. This is the second reason why Christians fall—they don't stay connected to him.

Ephesians 6:12 says, "For we wrestle not against flesh and blood, but against principalities, against powers, against the rulers of the darkness of this world, against spiritual wickedness in high places." Singularly, we mortals are flesh. Satan, on the other hand, is a spirit—a fallen, degenerate spirit. It stands to reason why man cannot fight a spirit with flesh. Flesh is dust—natural (mortal); spirit is supernatural (immortal). Yet it is the Holy Spirit in us who fights for us and through us in order to give us supernatural ability to victor over

Satan and our own (human or fleshly) limitations. So if you are not abiding in him (the Holy Spirit) when Satan (the evil spirit) comes against your flesh (the human, carnal spirit), you are not going to be able to hold him off. Consider the following scriptures:

> So I find this law at work: When I want to do good, evil is right there with me. For in my inner being I delight in God's law; but I see another law at work in the members of my body, waging war against the law of my mind and making me a prisoner of the law of sin at work in my members. What a wretched man I am! Who will rescue me from this body of death? Thanks be to God—through Christ Jesus our Lord! So then, I myself in my mind am a slave to God's law, but in the sinful nature a slave to the law of sin.
>
> Romans (7:21-25, NIV)

In John 15:1-7, Jesus said "remain in me" over five times in succession (NIV). Read it for yourself. He said if you want to live, "remain in me," if you want to bear fruit, "remain in me," if you want to bear much fruit, "remain in me," if you desire to prosper, "remain in me," and if you want your prayers answered, "remain in me." You see, our ability to remain erect (remember our definition of *falling*) is not secured by how many scriptures we know or the church we belong to; it's in our steadfast commitment to "remain in him." If we remain in Christ, we will be able to quickly identify our spiritual position and circumvent the temptation that ultimately leads to falling. Bottom line, people fall because they are not abiding in him.

Getting Back Up

> Brothers, if someone is caught in a sin, you who are spiritual should restore him gently. But watch for yourself, or you also may be tempted. Carry each other's burdens, and in this way you will fulfill the law of Christ. If anyone thinks he is something when he is nothing, he deceives himself.
>
> Galatians 6:1 (NIV)

Leaders, pastors, and preachers, our responsibility to the fallen is to restore them with love, forgiveness, and reconciliation. Most importantly, we must reposition them back into him. No doubt getting up and staying up is the most difficult task of all. Ordinarily, when one is caught in sin, the natural response is to run and hide. However, if anyone (humbly) submits himself before God, he will be healed and restored. Sometimes pride and stubbornness prevent us from getting the deliverance we need, but when we fall down, we need to stand down until we are fully recovered. Don't fool yourself; healing takes time. You must ensure you are not only well enough to get back up, but to get up and stay up. Again, rehabilitation is critical. You need to understand that. Those who move in haste, before they are completely healed, will eventually fall again. I call this principle the "rebound" effect.

The rebound effect occurs when an individual falls and before they are strong enough to stand on their own, they fall again. I can't help but wonder if Evangelist Swaggart would have avoided the second falling had he completely humbled himself to the leadership of the church and given himself time to recover. Ministers who fall and refuse to submit to the penalty mandated by the governing authorities of the church will either leave in disgrace or leave in rebellion. If they leave in disgrace, they will go to another church where nobody knows them and create a new identity. However, there is a problem with this philosophy. If they've failed to deal with the root of the matter, issues of a similar nature will eventually resurface. In other words, same problem, different day! On the other hand, those who leave in rebellion will proudly establish Ichabod assembly and say they are starting "a work for God." Of course, by reason of default, the foundation of the ministry can only be built with the materials provided by the founder—i.e. hate, rebellion, pride, deceit, jealousy, and disobedience. Lord, I shiver to think how many churches across the country have actually begun this way.

Releasing the Fallen

> If one falls down, his friend can help him up. But pity the man who falls and has no one to help him up!
>
> Ecclesiastes 4:10 (NIV)

At times, blind leaders piously close their eyes of compassion against fallen comrades. Perhaps their response is triggered by feelings of anger, betrayal, or disappointment. At any rate, it's still wrong. Sisters and brothers who fall and sincerely repent should be quickly reinstated into the fellowship of the church. Of course, this does not mean they should be allowed to pick up where they left off (depending on the weight of the offense, a sabbatical may be warranted). Nevertheless, it does mean they are still a welcomed addition to the family of God. Falling, no doubt, is bad enough, but falling without the aid and support of those who love you is even worse.

Since we already know that members of the body of Christ will fall, we must make every effort to hold them up. If they become discouraged and depressed, they are subject to go into hiding and walk away from the faith. Beloved, the acid test of your ministry is in your ability to love others through difficult times. As you began to minister to the fallen, remember this: "Love covers a multitude of sins" (1 Peter 4:7-8, NIV). Love is a healer. It transcends all rules and supersedes all boundaries. Therefore, if you can walk in love toward those who have fallen, grace will be shown to you if and when you're ever in a state of falling.

Review Precepts

1. Christians fall, no doubt about it; but if one continues to waddle in a cesspool of sin,

something is terribly wrong. Either they're bound by a demonic stronghold and need deliverance or (perhaps) they were never really saved in the first place.

2. Believers mustn't think they are immune to temptation and falling just because they are Christians. Regardless of your title or years of Christian experience, Satan desires to sift you as wheat, and he will patiently wait for you to approach a vulnerable moment in your life and pounce on you like a cheetah on a gazelle.

3. To avoid falling, saints must abide in Him. If we walk in the Spirit, we will not fulfill the lust of the flesh.

4. Whether a wound or injury was accidental or self-inflicted, the injured must undergo healing, sometimes emergency surgery, but definitely a period of rehabilitation.

5. No matter how embarrassing or demeaning the fall, one must stand down until they are really ready to stand up.

6. Leaders must make every attempt to revive, restore, and reconcile fallen foes. Undoubtedly, they need your love, patience, and genuine support.

Healing for the Spirit, Soul, and Body

*W*hy women think it is our job to rescue everyone, I will never know! Traditionally women around the globe disable the people in their lives by encouraging them to depend on them well beyond reasonable limits and expectations. Even as little girls, our parents subconsciously programmed us for self-neglect In many cases, as early as nine and ten years old, we were caring for siblings and manning household chores. Still, even as adults, we often find ourselves consuming the bulk of the dutiful responsibilities, including working outside of the home, participating in church and community activities, and nurturing the family.

So let me ask you a question. Are you the kind of person who constantly puts the needs of others before yourself? If your answer to this question is yes, when is a good time for you to start caring for you? Suppose I asked you to use three words to describe your reflexive (innate or automatic) response to the needs of other people. What three words would you use? Me, I would probably use such words as: dependable, trustworthy, and caring. I've discovered I frequently put the needs of others before myself because I feel remotely obligated to help them. Many women do that, and though that may not necessarily be a bad thing, it can become a problem if caring is not (at least on occasion) reciprocated toward oneself.

So now, let's do some self-reciprocation. Let's consider your own needs. Honestly speaking, tell me what three words you would use to describe your reflexive response to your own instinctive needs. Now, this may be a hypothetical assumption, but I would venture to say you'll describe your response to the needs of others with a more positive selection of words. Incidentally, the words you choose to use will determine whose needs are of most importance to you. Let's see if I'm correct. What three words did you use to describe your reflexive response to your own self needs? Me, I sadly selected the following: procrastination, inconsistent, and occasionally indolent. Umm! What do you think this simple exercise is suggesting? I believe it confirms the fact that women on average revere the needs of others over and above themselves.

Women naturally give much more than they receive, but is this really a good thing? What if she is giving and giving yet getting very little in return? John Gray, author of *Mars and Venus, Together Forever,* seems to agree. He explains, "It is a healthy feminine instinct for woman to give freely of themselves. Giving too much becomes a problem when a woman is not adept in getting back the nurturing support she needs to continue giving" (28).

Caring for Yourself

Based upon John Gray's comment and the results of the opening exercise, I'd simply say, Girls, you need a new attitude! If you spend all of your energy caring for other people, you are going to pass you by.

To experience life and live more abundantly, you must renew your mind and change your perspective on how you manage your oneness—yourself. Taking care of the woman in you is not wrong or selfish. It is an essential key to releasing enthusiasm, zest, and joy into your life and ministry. If you do not take the time to minister to you, your ministry, as well as your life, will greatly suffer. As I alluded to before, you cannot give what you do not have. Therefore, when you take the time to minister to you, you are empowering and strengthening yourself to ultimately care for others with minimal risk of burnout and fatigue. Once again, John Gray adds, "When a woman's female side is nurtured, her body begins to function naturally, and her exhaustion magically lifts" (29). God created you as a triune being. You are a spirit, you have a soul, and you live in a body, and every part of you needs specialized care and attention.

Many of us spend far too much time caring for others (family, church, school, job, etc.), and in the interim, we've failed to nourish and comfort the parts of us that keep us alive and functional. That, of course, includes a well-balanced diet, relaxation, exercise, some pampering, and laughter. When women, even Christian women, abuse their bodies and neglect its care, they are not exempt from serious, life-threatening diseases such as stroke, heart attack, obesity, and diabetes. Unfortunately, we are insidiously creating self-made martyrs.

Unbeknownst to some, self-neglect eventually transforms into feelings of resentment, bitterness, and entrapment, all of which could possibly be avoided if we'd simply listen to the cries from within. God designed our bodies with an internal indicator that automatically registers and detects high doses of stress and low doses of fresh air and water, soundness, and tranquility.

As a little girl, I grew up living in a small house with many different relatives, and my mother, bless her heart, was the custodian over everyone's care. She first cared for my older sister who both suffered from sickle cell anemia and was crippled as a result of the 1950's polio epidemic. Besides her, she nursed her ageing aunt. She unfortunately wrestled with bouts of geriatric dementia and hallucinations. Then she looked after my father's brother. He suffered from post-traumatic stress disorder and schizophrenia. And finally, she cared for us, my younger sister, father, and me. At any given time, all of us were living in the house together. My mother never got respite care. As a matter of fact, she didn't have a support system at all. She was an only child, no relatives—nothing; neither did she have the money to hire support, such as the likes of a private nurse or a trained medical assistant. So she bore the burden of nursing everyone alone.

I spent over twenty-two years living under my mother's roof, and I can only remember her taking two weekends off for a personal hiatus.

As a result of my mother's self-neglect, she eventually suffered two debilitating strokes that left her completely disabled, unable to walk or take care of herself. I learned a valuable lesson while watching my mother's somber demise: I don't want to do that! I don't want to care for others and in the process lose focus on caring for me.

To begin a self-care regimen, you must first venture into the central core of your personal being. Of course, I'm not suggesting new-age exercises, meta-physical enlightenment, or self-actualization of the mind (though I may refer to similar-sounding terms). No, I'm limpidly referring to using basic Bible principles to master internal reflections, meditation skills, and motion (movement). Subsequently, this chapter addresses many self-care issues. Prayerfully, you will discover how these healing tips interlocking as one may be necessary for the success and existence of the other.

Internal Reflection

Without fail, no matter how painful it may be, at the beginning of the New Year I force myself to pause and reflect on the accomplishments and failures of the previous year. With truth as evidence, I put myself on the witness stand and cross examine my heart. The first principle of internal reflections is truth. In order to be set free (in any area of your life), you must sincerely embrace and acknowledge the truth. The Bible says, "And ye shall know the truth, and the truth shall make you free" (John 8:32, KJV). Unfortunately, too many believers are in self-denial, crouching behind plastic smiles, when in reality they do not know who they are. Nor do they know or understand the integral workings of their own spirit, mind, and body. In fact, they are completely alienated from the reality of the truth within.

In Genesis 32:22-32, Jacob wrestled all night with an angel at the ford of Jabbok. At daybreak, the angel was forced to disable Jacob's grip by touching him in the hollow of his hip. Even with a disabling limp, Jacob insisted as he spoke with the angel, "I will not let you go until you bless me!" The angel replied, "I cannot bless you until you tell me your name." What the angel really wanted from Jacob was an acknowledged confession of truth. "Reveal your true identity and tell me who you really are." Once Jacob revealed his true self, the angel was at liberty to release the blessing upon him.

Much like Jacob, many of us deny the truth within and, in turn, find ourselves delaying needful change. Yet we have the audacity to wrestle with God for the external blessing we want and think we deserve.

Some saints have masked the truth so long that reality is literally unrecognizable. Nevertheless, to experience true deliverance, we must challenge ourselves to acknowledge the sounds within and to deal with them honestly, appropriately, and expeditiously.

> The word of God is quick, and powerful, and
> sharper than any two-edged sword, piercing
> even to the dividing asunder of soul and spirit,
> and of the joints and marrow, and is a discerner
> of the thoughts and intents of the heart.
>
> Hebrews 4:12 (KJV)

Consequently, if you will challenge yourself and confront yourself about you, nothing will prohibit your deliverance. God has given us the power to heal ourselves through the word of God. In so doing, we have the authority within us to override the enemy, to heal the broken places in our spirits, and to release ourselves to walk in freedom. Again, I don't want you to misinterpret what I'm saying. This is not mind over matter or "self-god theology." It is simply taking the principles in the Word of God and willfully submitting them to your own human spirit until the power of God is completely transformed in you—spirit, mind, and body. It's as easy as this: "So if the Son sets you free, you will be free indeed" (John 8:36, NIV).

Words of Affirmation

Affirmation is an important technique in exercising internal reflections. You should practice on a daily basis speaking words that will encourage your spirit, mind, and body. I assure you it will completely change your life. Sometimes you have to remind yourself that you're blessed and highly favored.

Through the power of positive confession, we can take the word of God and command life to exist, even in situations and circumstances that were previously barren and desolate. The Bible says, "The tongue has the power of life and death, and those who love it will eat its fruit" (Proverbs 18:21, NIV). I consistently divorce myself from negativism by dismissing thoughts of failure, loss, and defeat.

Every day we are surrounded by negative influences, be they from the television, radio, gossip columnist, newspapers, magazine tabloids, or the Internet. In most cases, even our own personal conversations are often melancholy and depressing. Have there been instances in your life when everything around you seemed to affirm negativism? In my case, it began with the weather. Let me explain. When we first moved to England, the weather (which is often wet, dreary, and cold), frequently caused me to feel depressed. As you can imagine, I'd often find myself whining and complaining—"Blah, blah, blah. I have no friends! I have no job!" After awhile, I got tired of submitting to my own mouth and emotions, and I took control over my confession. Soon after, the depressive feelings began to subside. It was quite simple; all I had to do was change my confession. Instead of sitting in the house, complaining, I started voicing an appreciation for life—Zoe life (the God kind of life).

To my surprise, beauty was everywhere. As I began to search for it, I'd find it in the most unexpected places. Yes, in everything we must learn how to give thanks.

Likewise, as it relates to people. I disconnect myself from negative people. The motivational speaker Les Brown called negative people "energy drainers." Mr. Brown cautions us on the dangers of energy drainers. He says, "These are the kind of people who rob you of your peace and steal your joy." Saints, don't let people contaminate your spirit. Believe the Lord's report: If God said it, he'll do it. If he spoke it, he'll bring it too pass. *Selah*!

If you are interested in learning some positive affirmations, I would suggest you purchase a promise book. Promise books are filled with scriptures that incite life confessions. They are usually very inexpensive, quick to reference, and a thrifty tool to help you learn how to memorize scriptures.

Quieting the Spirit Within

> But I have stilled and quieted my soul; like a weaned child with its mother, like a weaned child is my soul within me.
>
> Psalm 131:2 (NIV)

Whether you are in the elevator at your favorite department store or crossing a busy intersection in New York City, noise is all around you. Noises can either be comforting and soothing or disturbing and distracting. Although we don't always have control over the external noises within our environment, we can take control of the internal noises within our spirits. Consequently, in order to turn off the noises in your spirit, you must first locate and dismantle the negative feeders. There are many kinds of internal and external feeders. Yet they exist as a means of opposing your peace.

Recently I attended a women's retreat where the facilitator asked us to quiet our spirits for one hour. That meant no radio, no television, no talking, nothing—complete silence. After the hour had ended and we rejoined for the general session, she asked the group how they felt about the quite time activity. Some said, "I almost went crazy not talking," while others said, "I just decided to go to my room and go to sleep so the hour would go by faster." Only a few of us took advantage of the serenity.

The activity was not intended to cause anxiety, but because many of the women were not accustomed to quieting their spirit, they were greatly annoyed. As a result, they failed to benefit from the solace and peace provided in the activity.

Moreover, a healthy mind and body doesn't camp in modes of repeat and rewind; it stops, rests, and then restarts. Otherwise, it will never recuperate and heal itself appropriately.

Negative feeders such as worry, unforgiveness, indecisiveness, gossip, and rejection must be apprehended and drenched with massive doses of truth, love, positive confessions, and the uncompromising word of God. If not, they can and will take full control of your life. Negative feeders can be controlled, but it takes a conscious effort to do so. Instead of positivism, we humans by nature feed on negativism. Therefore, to change our behavior, we must change our mentality. With that in mind, our actions will in time begin to bear witness to that confession.

Meditation

After the death of Moses, the Lord chose Joshua, son of Nun, as his ardent successor. I would think in some way or another Joshua may have personally felt dwarfed in the shadow of Moses's zenith accomplishments. After all, Moses's legacy vividly affirmed his stellar performance. Nevertheless, God told Joshua to be strong and very courageous. In comforting him, he instructed him to meditate on the word both day and night so he too would prosper and have good success (Joshua 1:8). In order to prevent discouragement and self-defeat, God wanted Joshua to consistently ponder and think on good things—God things.

As it relates to meditation, Christians don't sit on the floor with their eyes closed and their legs crossed chanting "umm, umm." Nor do we "direct our energies" by thinking about or ruminating on "cosmic forces, auras, and higher powers." When we centralize our thoughts, we think on the omniscient, omnipotent, and omnipresence of God at work in our own personal lives and ministries. We do as the scriptures teach us; we "put on the mind of Christ" by thinking on those things which are from above:

> Finally, brothers, whatever is true, whatever is noble, whatever is right, whatever is pure,

whatever is lovely, whatever is admirable— if anything is excellent or praiseworthy—think about such things.

Philippians 4:8 (NIV)

Meditate is defined by Webster as "to think upon, to ponder, to muse over, or to contemplate." Meditation is a mental exercise that allows you to take the word of God and gain control over your mind and thoughts. Ordinarily, temptation begins with a single thought. Therefore, if we train our minds to bring our thoughts under subjection, we can control mental traffic and curtail demonic intrusion (2 Corinthians 10:4-5).

Meditation will teach you how to focus on the word of God. Again, if meditation is to be rewarding and beneficial, you must focus and concentrate on him, not yourself or what you're planning to cook for dinner, but on him and the relationship you share with him. When you truly know who God is and who he is in your personal life, thinking about him comes easily. Furthermore, by continually speaking and "muddling over" the word of God in your spirit, you are becoming more learned in the scriptures and more fortified in your spirit, mind, and body.

Journaling: A Tool of Expression

Simple or fancy, I really like journals. I will buy a journal for anyone on any occasion. I happen to think journals make the perfect gift, and they're never out of season. For me, writing is a personal solace that treats me like the old 70s commercial for Calgon: "it takes me away." Although journaling may not be for everyone, it is a great way to relax and practice writing your positive affirmations.

I usually have about three journals going at any given time. For one, I keep a church journal. That journal contains my sermons, messages, and Bible study notes. Then I have a journal that is filled with my favorite words and quotes. I enjoy composing quotations and collecting words. Finally, I have a personal journal. And believe you me, there's no telling what's in that one. I tell that journal all of my secrets, disappointments, dreams, and personal aspirations.

Another positive aspect of journaling is recording reflections, prayer requests, and prophecies. It would be ideal if we could remember everything God tells us in prayer or perhaps shows us in our dreams. However, if you train yourself to write things down, you'll be less likely to forget them. Journaling serves to remind you of God's promise. It is a manuscript revealing when, where, and how he fulfilled the prophecy and/or answered your prayer. In a more practical way, a journal can also help you manage your time by keeping you abreast of meetings, appointments, and other important activities.

Redefining Your Environment

My husband has this thing about "environmental stress." Consequently, when the dishes are unwashed and piles of dirty laundry line the floor, it's only a matter of time before the soldier in him rises to the occasion. From the oldest to the youngest, everybody is ordered to apprehend a handy device (a mop, a rag, a broom, a vacuum cleaner, or anything) just get busy, and proceed with caution.

Nevertheless, when things begin to pile up in corners, closets, storage spaces, trash cans, under beds, and over beds, you are seriously being invaded by environmental stress. Did you not know that your environment has everything to do with your health and mental wellness? You can't take charge of your life if you don't take charge of your environment.

You can do this by going from room to room, perhaps on a day off or on a holiday break, and de-clutter and free up available space. I understand this is a sacrifice, but when it's all said and done, it'll be well worth the effort. At the same time, if you are really inspired, you can take it a step farther. Forfeit a few unnecessary outfits and invest in some plastic storage bins and closet organizers. You will definitely feel more control over your life if your life space is not overwhelmed by trash.

Your environment will promote or prohibit inner healing. Consequently, internal wellness and peace is directly connected to your five senses, and each of them are capable of detecting and registering intrusive elements. Quite commonly, certain odors can either cure you or kill you.

Case in point, Jonathan, my oldest son, likes to play basketball—a lot! Yet he had a terrible habit of taking off his dirty gym gear and throwing it in the closet, causing his room to smell like armpits and feet. After about a week or two, the clothes would begin to decompose, sending a foul, unattractive scent throughout the house. Immediately, upon unlocking the front door, the smell would rush down the stairs and apprehend you like a bandit. As you can only imagine, the decaying garments were very easy to locate. I knew exactly where the evidence was buried. Now my world was being inhabited by environmental stress, and the response was urgent: 911, get this stinky stuff washed, now! Meanwhile, for just a tattered moment, my senses had been altered. The odor had shattered the tranquil atmosphere in which I breathed by disturbing my internal balance and peace. I was no longer the happy, sound, and internally quieted sister in the Lord. I was mad! My son has finished college now and is preparing for law school, but his little brother, Ernest Jr., has decided he wants to continue the tradition of the brotherhood—basketball and decaying gym gear.

In the end, you must take responsibility for your environment. It is the healing balm to your soul. Bringing your life to order is a gift you give to yourself because you cannot effectively minister to others when your life is in chaos and disarray.

Love Your Body

We women are our hardest critics. We complain about our eyes, skin, hair, hips, nose… you name it, we don't like it. Magazine and tabloid ads encourage us to chronically diet and budget for Botox treatments.

Nevertheless, being thin and wrinkle free does not constitute the model for beauty and wellness.

The proverbs woman serves as a classical example of the characteristics of a beautiful woman. She is a lady with a quieted spirit, whole, complete, and comfortable with herself and the woman within. This assumption is evident by the response of those within her "life circle" (we will define *life circle* in the next chapter). In her honor, the Bible says, "Her children arise and call her blessed: her husband also, and he praises her" (Proverbs 31:28, NIV).

This woman is clearly at peace with herself, and that's the confidence that makes her alluring. Although the Bible does not describe her physical features, whatever she may have looked like didn't hinder her from being *femme par excellence*, a stellar entrepreneur, mother, wife, and friend.

Women who love themselves regardless of body structure usually have a more defined and pronounced core, as they are also balanced in other areas in their lives as well. Women who struggle with self-love issues are unhappy, contentious, angry, and difficult to please.

Hurting women express their pain in many different ways. Unfortunately, disgruntled women attack themselves with crippling, harsh, and self-destructive words. In fact, they frequently entertain feelings of self-hatred, and it's played out in their choice of friends, mates, and decisions. In addition, these sisters are equally capable of lashing out at the people closest to her. Women who struggle with self-love issues seldom find solace within themselves. Surprisingly enough, you can lose weight, visit the beauty parlor, and buy a new outfit, but if you don't change your attitude about yourself, then the aesthetics are simply worthless. Bottom line: if you can't love yourself at your worst, you'll find a reason not to love yourself at your best.

This is an interesting phenomenon; however, I've counseled women who admit to loving God and others but hating themselves. Learning to love yourself begins with accepting who you are. Frankly speaking, you can't really appreciate the pleasures of life until you learn how to love and appreciate yourself.

Do you own a full-length mirror? If you do, I'd like for you to take a moment to look at yourself. What do you see? What initially draws you to your image? Hopefully it's the feature(s) you like. While you're gazing at your stature, don't forget to look into your heart. There you will find your internal features, features such as kindness, gentleness, patience, integrity, and sincerity.

Now, what about the features you don't like (both inside and out)? What are you going to do about them? Keep in mind while some things about you can be changed, others things, however, cannot. Your height, for example, is permanent—you can't change that. On the other hand, your attitude and disposition is spiritual—*that* you can change.

Nevertheless, I can offer you a sensible solution. If your disdain or dislike isn't in your power to fix it or change it, put a bow on it and call it a day. But if you really don't like what you see, and it's in your power to change it, stop talking about it and take action. Get the help you need to empower yourself to move. At any rate, don't contaminate your spirit with negativism and self-hatred (1 Peter 3:1-5).

Rest and Relaxation

Another important area in holistic care is rest and relaxation. On average, people these days don't get a normal rest. With so much to do in the process of a day, many are so wired by the time they physically stop they're mentally incapable of shutting down the system and naturally unwinding. As a result, some find themselves soliciting the aid of substances such as alcohol, drugs, or sex to induce a simulated rest. Nevertheless, rest and relaxation is essentially important to the overall healing of your spirit, soul, and body.

To enjoy rest and relaxation, you have to actually stop and slow your body down. Interestingly enough, rest and relaxation is not the same as internal reflections or meditation. However, you must slow yourself down in order to participate in those activities as well. At any rate, rest and relaxation means more than just stopping. It means to consciously leave the cares of the day behind and do something you really enjoy doing. Moreover, when you relax, though you may be busy and attentive, you are physically and mentally disengaged and abated. My kids would call it "chillin'."

Me? I enjoy reading. When I can get in a sudsy bath with a good book and a hot cup of English tea, or perhaps a cold Diet Pepsi (depending on my mood), I'm absolutely at peace. Everyone in the whole house knows my routine, and they respectfully honor my time. My family has learned how to appreciate my "me time" because they know if I can get away for a few relaxing moments, I will be a better mom and wife. Beloved, you owe it to yourself. So take a few minutes everyday for a little rest and relaxation.

The Great Get Away

Years ago, psychologists devised a profile to help individuals understand their instinctive response(s) to everyday stressors. The test was called a personality profile. My personality profile suggests that I am a healthy, happy, well-balanced, type-B individual. Yet under stressful conditions, conditions such as those induced as a result of "yes projects" (I'll explain that concept later), I have the propensity to rapidly convert to a borderline type A. Consequently, my husband knows my mood tends to vacillate under extended pressure, so from time to time he would send me away on what I called a "post-project hiatus."

A few years ago, I was working on this particular "yes project" (anything you say yes to knowing full well you do not have the time or the energy to support). It was slaying me. Fortunately, my husband was scheduled for a business trip in Hawaii, so he bought me a ticket and asked me to go with him. I knew I really needed the break, so I eagerly agreed to go. To my surprise, this particular trip turned out to be nothing less than transforming. Although I have been to Hawaii many times before, this time I really experienced the healing properties of rest and relaxation.

We stayed at the elegant Hale Koa Military Resort in Honolulu, and the view from our hotel room was absolutely breathtaking. Every morning for two days, I got up early and watched the sun introduce itself to a brand-new day.

One morning before the break of dawn, I decided I wanted to see the sunrise from the beach, so I ventured down to the pier. Once I got to the water's edge, I sat down in the sand and closed my eyes. Slowly I tilted my head back in serenity as I felt the tide push warm sudsy water beneath my feet. After which I listened attentively as the waves boldly crashed against the rocks. God's presence overtook me, and I began to weep. The beauty of his magnificent creation was all around me, and I didn't have to see it to know it was there. Surely to the Pacific Islanders, my child-like experience was in and of itself simply the norm. But to me, it was absolutely awe inspiring. All in all, I was instantly restored and rejuvenated as I enclosed myself in God's majestic splendor.

You may not be able to go all the way to Hawaii to get some rest (restoration) and relaxation, but by all means, go somewhere. God's beauty is all around us, and it is indeed a wonder to behold. So plan a date with nature. Have your lunch in the park underneath the trees or sit on your back porch at sunset and watch the night consume the light of the day. You can achieve the same healing experience if you'll just get away and make it happen.

Laughter

> A cheerful heart is good medicine, but a crushed
> spirit dries up the bones.
>
> Proverbs 17:22 (NIV)

Finally, I'll share my last healing tip for this chapter—laughter. Some people act as though laughter and letting go is a sin. On the contrary, laughter is quite healing; it warms the heart and cheers the spirit.

I've been married for twenty-eight years, and, though I liked many things about my husband when I first meet him, his finest asset was his ability to make me laugh. He could (and I might add *still can*) make a joke out of anything. In fact, no matter how serious or somber the subject, he can find a pinch of humor in it.

Although I'm not much of a fan for TV watching, my husband really enjoys old sitcoms like *The Andy Griffith Show* and *The Honeymooners*. Many times, I'd be in my quiet corner with a good book and a hot cup of tea, and he would be in front of the big-screen TV, laughing at Barney Fife and Ernest T. Bass. He'd be laughing so hard I'd have to put my book down and go check on him. Overall, my family is a jovial bunch; in fact, from time to time, we'll sit together and construct our own rendition of *Dinner and a Movie*. It's really a lot of fun.

Nevertheless, there is still a more healing form of laughter, and that is the ability to laugh at *yourself*. No matter how embarrassing it may be, you must admit that when your weave falls off during an exhilarating praise and worship experience—that's funny. It's also funny when your pantyhose roll down around the lower part of your thighs while you're standing in the frozen food section of the grocery store. So what must you do? Laugh and laugh a lot. Listen, you can't take yourself too seriously. Learn to appreciate the silly stuff. When God inspired me to write this book, I knew I had to cushion it with humor because so much of the content was serious. It is my desire that every reader finish this book enlightened, encouraged, inspired, and laughing! Laughter is good, healing, and therapeutic.

By the way, the laugh-out-loud examples I previously mentioned actually happened to me.

Review Precepts

1. Tending to your own personal needs is very important. Women must practice taking the time to minister to themselves.

2. Caring for others is an automatic reflexive response in most women. However, balancing the two, self and others, must be a continual ritual; otherwise fatigue, exhaustion, and resentment will follow.

3. Who are you? Do you really know who you are? If you will honestly address you about you, you will discover things about yourself you may not be aware of. Some believers spend so much time

making excuses for their inconsistencies they never actually face or confront their reality.

4. Meditation and words of affirmation are tools that actually soothe and pamper the soul. Both are a needful practice that's frequently disregarded.

5. Many people like background noise because they don't want to adhere or submit to their inner conscience. It's much easier to drown the silence with music, television, shopping, partying, gossip, sexual conquest, etc. However, God visits those who'll "stand still" and quiet their spirit long enough to hear his voice.

6. Your spirit can laugh, live, release, and rest if your life space is clutter free—not just your natural living quarters, but your mind, emotions, body, decisions, finances, business, relationships, habits, schedule, appetites, family life, and last but not least, your ministry.

Sister Love

*I*n the previous chapter, we discussed the value of caring for ourselves through positive affirmations, relaxation, and laughter. Now we are ready to share the love—women ministering to women. In almost every instance, when sisters care for sisters, it's demonstrated through the sisterhood of friendship. Nothing illustrates brotherly love like girl friends. If women dare to release themselves to love and be loved, they will faithfully support, adhere, and connect themselves to every relationship they bond to.

Learning to give and receive love is very difficult for some women to do. Nevertheless, if a genuine covenant of fellowship is formed, it will last a lifetime. There are four expressions of love in the Greek:

- *Agape* love: this is the God kind of love that is unwavering and unconditional.

- *Storge* love: this love denotes natural affection, similar to that felt by a parent for his or her children.

- *Phila* or *phileo* love: this is brotherly love that is heart felt but sometimes circumstantial.

- *Eros* love: this is a sensual or an erotic expression of love.

Most of us are familiar with the demonstration of storge, philia, and eros love. But agape love is God's love, and only he can show us how to emulate that. In fact, without agape love, it is impossible to genuinely express philia love toward others, especially for those who are difficult to embrace. Nevertheless, women everywhere long to build strong sister-to-sister relationships whereby they can safely share conversation, support, and comradeship. However, in order for them to release themselves to freely participate and embrace the core of the relationship, they need to see agape and philia love demonstrated in concert.

When Jesus lived among the disciples, he demonstrated the union of agape and philia love. He tells us as he told them, love one another as "I have loved you" (John 15:12, KJV). Love is the mark of true discipleship. Regardless of our differences, personalities, or temperament, we are obligated to reach out in faith and touch and embrace one another. Sister love is but one of the many ways we can celebrate the true covenant of Christian friendship. True sister love motivates, encourages, stimulates, and emulates the love of Christ.

Defining the Circles

There are three kinds of circles identified in this book— four if you consider yourself as a circle or an entity unto itself. They are defined as the inner circle (close friends), the life circle (family), and the outer circle (all others).

If you think of these circles like the rotation of planets in the solar system, you will better understand how the alignment of your personal circles affect the way you interact with others. Like the sun that sits in the center of the universe, everyone in your circle or circles rotates or revolves around you. Each level, or sphere, represents a different degree of intimacy. Obviously, those closest to the self circle (or the sun) will absorb the most heat.

Coincidentally, every person in your world, collectively yet at varying degrees, makes up your outer circle. Thus, the outer circle is the first and largest circle.

Then we have the life circle. The life circle represents the lineage from which you were born. In fact, every member in your family (both far and near) make up your life circle. We don't always have the privilege of selecting the members or individuals born or adopted within our life circle. Yet these are the people who have the greatest amount of power and influence over our lives. Those within our life circle are usually close to us in proximity but not necessarily in intimacy.

The most rewarding circle of all is by far the inner circle. The inner circle represents those individuals who are intimately connected to you. They are the people you've privileged and personally invited to share in your life's journey. Trust and faithfulness are tantamount in the inner circle, as they are above all else the glue that perpetually bonds its members to a true covenant of friendship. Like Jonathan and David, inner circle relationships are established among those of like faith, "iron sharpening iron" (Proverbs 27:17, NIV).

Why Are Circles Important?

> While Jesus was still talking to the crowd, his mother and brothers stood outside, wanting to speak to him. Someone told him, "Your mother and brothers are standing outside, wanting to speak to you." He replied to him, "Who is my mother, and who are my brothers?" Pointing to his disciples, he said, "Here are my mother and my brothers. For whoever does the will of my Father in heaven is my brother and sister and mother.
>
> Matthew 12:46-50 (NIV)

It is important for you to identify those within your various circles by learning how to value and appreciate the contributions each one brings to the relationship. Who will you entrust with the rights to the inner circle? And who by reason of sensibility and wisdom is reserved to the outer circle? Everyone within your circles interface and intertwine. Moreover, they pass over and through your life like the moon obscures the sun during an eclipse. Yet as we identify the importance of those within these various realms, we are able to dispense our energies more efficiently.

For instance, inner-circle relationships offer mutual interaction and social exchange. Therefore if personal time is weaned and depleted, it's usually quite acceptable. Family, those within your life circle, will usually consume the bulk of your time and energy. However, in all honesty, you may or may not appreciate the time loss. Meanwhile, individuals positioned within the outer circle, the largest realm, receive attention and fellowship based upon their specific needs. Responsibilities to individuals within the outer circle are not only minimal but are also relative.

If you're still questioning the importance of this information, consider the fact that some women have a tendency to misinterpret or misunderstand the depth of intimacy released and expressed at various levels within a relationship. Therefore, understanding your circles and where each individual in your circle fits, you will be able to minimize or perhaps even eliminate interpersonal confusion.

Although our love should always depict equality, the level of personal and social intimacy we demonstrate is based upon one's assigned circle and the proximity of each individual person. This is where agape love truly resonates. Thus, agape love helps us circumvent our own needs, desires, biases, inhibitions, and comfort zones in light of reaching others and bringing them in closer to the self circle. This, of course, does not mean that every person brought in close belongs to the inner circle. No, it simply means positioning them for ministry by bringing them close enough for you to share God's love with them. Who are these people? Well, they are your coworkers, neighbors, your child's teacher, or the clerk at your favorite grocery store.

Ideally, you'll always be positioned close to the farthest end of your outer circle. That way, as strange as it may seem to onlookers, the doors of opportunity are always open, bridging agape and phileo love together in concert.

The Inner Circle

No doubt the most important people in your life are those within your inner circle. Jesus, knowing the ambivalence in the hearts of the people, carefully assessed the motives of those within his various circles. Who were the true followers and who were the imposters? Even though Jesus had many disciples, it was the three, Peter, James, and John, in whom he became most affectionate. These three men were a part of Jesus's inner circle, and he gave them the privilege of knowing him up close and personal. As a matter of fact, they alone witnessed Jesus's miraculous transformation on the mountain of transfiguration (Matthew 17:1-12). As it stood, none of the other disciples accompanied him on this glorious event. So should we assume they were not as important to him as the other three men? I think not. Simply put, inner-circle relationships reveal a deeper sphere of intimacy.

These particular factors are based upon characteristics such as trust, history, purpose, loyalty, integrity, and covenant. Why are inner-circle relationships so important? And why should we value and cherish them above all others? Well, let's consider a few amazing facts:

- First of all, inner-circle relationships offer true friendship. Preachers tend to forget they really need to develop true, genuine relationships.

- Inner circle partners are true soul sisters. Like soul mates, they know you by the Spirit and love you with the Spirit.

- Inner-circle partners are not looking for anything special from you; they are actively involved with the mutual exchange received within the relationship.

- Inner-circle partners can be trusted. They are loyal confidants who like Jonathan risked his own life for his friend David.

- Inner-circle partners are few in number. You may have many wonderful people in your life, but the inner circle is finite.

- Inner-circle partners will tell you the truth about yourself. These people honestly desire to help you stay balanced. Beloved, you don't need to be around people who constantly flatter and feed your ego. When you're wrong, you're wrong, and somebody in your life should be permitted to tell you.

- Inner-circle partners are nonjudgmental. These people see you in the worst of times but love you anyway.

- Inner-circle partners know when you need prayer—yes and amen, even before you ask.

- Inner-circle relationships are spiritual. They are not superficial and fleshly.

- Inner-circle relationships are not taxing, cumbersome, or overbearing—personal space is highly respected.

- Inner-circle partners are people that respect your self-circle. They don't get offended when you need time alone.

Bringing the Outer Circle in Closer

Any time you bring people reserved to the outer circle to close to the inner circle or self-circle, you stand the risk of straining the relationship. Nevertheless, the closer you position others to your self-circle, the more personal your relationships become. On average, it is not always easy to pull sisters into a closer realm of proximity to yourself.

History suggests that women commonly share conversation and fellowship as a means of connecting themselves to other sister love supporters. In John Gray's book *Mars and Venus Together Forever* he says this about women: "Talking about problems, sharing feelings, and articulating desires became a feminine ritual to create greater intimacy and express loyalty to the community" (43). Even though sister-sister fellowship is essential and greatly desired, women still exclude themselves from the exchange. There are many different reasons why this is so. The more common reason perhaps is for feelings of distrust, skepticism, or fear, all of which overwhelmingly preclude sister-to-sister bonding. In fact, many sister-sister relationships are wrecked even before they begin—all because of preconceived ideas.

One day Jesus met a woman at Samaria's well. Her story is told in John 4. Customarily, Jews gathered at the well early in the morning and late in the evening to not only fetch water but to fellowship and converse with one another. This woman, however, was not only a minority (a non-Jew) but a woman with an unscrupulous lifestyle. So to divert embarrassment and shame, she guarded her heart, avoided the women, and ventured to the well in the middle of the day. In light of her past history, she knew communing with the other women would be risky and foolish. "What if they start asking me questions about my husband or my children? What will I say?" Bottom line, she dared not take a chance at intermingling or "shooting the breeze" with the other woman. She knew she had nothing in common with them, nor were they exceptionally drawn to her and her revolting disposition.

Ah! But little did she know her past was about to become the catalyst to her future. Her lifestyle may have initially caused the other women to shun her, but deep down inside, she was not who they thought she was. In fact, she was not who she thought she was. She was much more than her problems and issues, and that fact became apparently obvious once she met Jesus Christ. When she came in contact with him, her reputation was no longer of consequence. She dismissed her shame and ran through the city, boldly proclaiming Jesus Christ as Lord.

First, we must realize we are sisters in Christ, regardless of our history, differences, and/or similarities. For sister-love relationships to essentially provide spiritual healing and internal cleansing, we've first got to practice and understand this principle. Our sisters' deliverance depends upon their willingness to open up, repent, and release the poison. The Bible says, "Therefore confess your sins to each other and pray for each other so that you may be healed. The prayer of a righteous man is powerful and effective" (James 5:16, NIV).

To bring the outer circle closer, you must construct healthy relationships. Paul admonishes us to build relationships with spiritual materials, so the foundation therein can withstand the pressures of adversity and change. You'll find the closer you get to Christ, the more you'll outgrow certain people and relationships altogether.

In fact, as you spiritually mature, you will eventually desire a true (covenant) sister-love relationship. This desire is based upon a different set of needs—spiritual needs. As you well know, relationships built on temporal factors soon lead to disappointing ends. Eventually, signs of pettiness, envy, and selfishness emerge, dismantling the entire relationship. We've all seen it before, sisters publicly heralding irrational, loose, and irresponsible comments toward one another. Slowly but surely, a silent wall of shame and embarrassment assembles between them. Once the drama finally subsides, the sisters are left with feelings of anger, betrayal, hurt, and ultimately, bitterness. Mark my words, its demonic and fleshly in nature.

Dealing with Issues of Distrust

Every woman knows what it feels like to be betrayed. At some point in time, someone you thought was a friend divulged your trust and exposed your secrets. Now you feel vulnerable, unable to respond to genuine sister-love support. Traditionally, when women suffer with issues of distrust, it is very difficult for them to open up and share with others. Women, even those within the sanctuary of the church, don't always feel safe and protected amongst other women. Sad to say, but for some, their worst offenses were funneled through the hands of church-going people. When sisters lack wisdom and moral discretion, they can, even by accident, fatally wound other sisters.

Gossip and back biting is probably the biggest obstacle to sister-sister bonding. Thus, any information that is shared with you in confidence should be reserved for you, the listener, and the listener only. Sisters, if you have never been at the caboose of such devilish dialogue, consider yourself blessed, because I'm here to tell you it's very painful. An old church mother once told me, "The same dog that brings a bone carries a bone," and judging from past experiences, she was right.

One thing is certain: women will not share their intimate secrets with women they do not trust to preserve their confidentiality. The Bible says in Proverbs 18:24, "A man that hath friends must shew himself friendly. and there is a friend that sticketh closer than a brother" (kjv). It is true: to have friends, you must show yourself friendly. Nevertheless, being friendly is not enough; you must also show yourself to be trustworthy. Most women would rather have one friend they can trust than a host of friends who are untrustworthy.

Making New Friends

If distrust becomes a factor in any given relationship, fear is soon to follow, and fear in and of itself is tormenting. In consequence, fear will hinder you from doing those things you know you are supposed to do. Perhaps at this very moment there are sisters in your outer circle you know God has told you to invite into a closer proximity to you. Yet for fear you've turned them away, never knowing what could become of the relationship. Women everywhere have the same response to this dilemma: "What if I start to trust her and she stabs me in the back?" Regardless of one's intentions, fear of the unknown will ultimately prevent you from coming into a closer relationship with other women (or anyone else for that matter). Fear is a spirit, and it must be handled in the spirit realm.

You can reduce the fear in relationship building if you learn how to identify the characteristics of a spiritually based relationship. First of all, you can't be "wishy-washy." In everything let your "yea be yea and your nay be nay" (James 5:12, KJV). Why would you expect others to be honest and forthcoming if you are not? Jesus said, "For whoever does the will of my Father in heaven is my brother and sister and mother" (Matthew 12:50, NIV). Therefore, the first characteristic of relationship building is a mutual love for the things of God. Amos 3:3 says, "Do two walk together unless they have agreed to do so?" (NIV). When you meet someone you think you'd like to share a lasting relationship with, you need to ask yourself these questions: Was the connection between us spiritual or carnal? What do we really have in common? and What do I really know about this person and their walk with the Lord? Am I willing to let God direct and cultivate this relationship?

As a minister of the gospel, I've learned the importance of carefully assessing the character of those within my circles. In fact, I attentively look for signs of godly fruit. Rarely, if ever, will I bond with someone before I've had the opportunity to discern their level of spirituality. This solemn determination must be made beforehand since their level of maturity has everything to do with their position of proximity to me.

That is why I believe this message is of such great importance, especially to lady preachers, because problems arise when sisters bond with sisters who are spiritually immature. As a minister of the gospel, it is your job to teach, instruct, encourage, reprove, and lead God's women in their spiritual growth and development. And that's very difficult to do if you're trying to be their friend and running buddy.

Ministering to Women in General

It is comforting to know not all women are looking for a sister-sister relationship. Some sisters are simply looking for a mentor in the faith. Understand, when women come into your life, they come for many different reasons. Some want to be touched by you and your ministry, some want a friend and social companion, some want you to give them pomp and position, and some want to be a blessing to you and your ministry. At any rate, those who come to receive ministry must be dealt with on a ministry scale. Ask yourself, "What do they need from me, and what am I willing to give?"

Not every sister is looking for someone to fix their problems. Some sisters just want a sympathetic supporter. More often than not, sisters just want someone to care. "To care" often means to listen. To actively listen, you must do more than hear with understanding; you must purpose to process what's said without passing judgment or making premature assumptions.

On the other hand, "faith without works is dead" (James 2:26, KJV). Therefore, there are times when we must do more than listen to one another's problems. We must exemplify our faith by offering our support. Gary Chapman, author of *The Five Love Languages*, makes an interesting assessment regarding "expressions of love" in relationships. Whereas his book was primarily written to enhance communication among married couples, the principles therein can apply to any love relationship, including sister-sister. I'll briefly explain what I mean.

The first language of love is words of affirmation. Sisters need to hear words of encouragement. Some sisters rarely, if ever, hear kind, supportive words, and your words of solace and comfort can heal the most damaged heart. When we speak words of life to one another, we heal one another and inspire support.

Secondly, there is quality time. When quality time is used as a language of love, we learn how to effectively utilize the time spent with other sisters. Thus, we don't waste precious moments discussing unhealthy topics. No, we use our time to build one another up in the faith.

The third language of love is giving and receiving of gifts. Although this may be a tangible expression of love and kindness, what counts in the long run are the matters of the heart, not the amount of money spent. I believe it is the little things that often mean the most.

Now the forth love language, acts of service, is actually my favorite. In fact, I'm at my very best when I'm able to give my service to others. Because I happen to admire this language above all others, I tend to think it yields the greatest benefit to sisters in need.

The final love language is physical touch. Everybody needs a hug, and sometimes the soft comforting touch of another sister can make all the difference in a traumatically hectic day.

Now, I've illustrated below some of the ways I like to express love. Comparing your expressions of love to my list, which love language do you think you probably utilize most often? How do you express that love to other sisters?

- Watching the children for the day.
- Offering to pay for a manicure and/or pedicure.
- Taking a sister out to dinner and/or a movie.

- Reading a good book together with a discussion party to follow.
- Praying and studying the word together.
- Sending a sister flowers or a cheerful card.
- Surprising a sister with her favorite sweet treat.
- Buying a sister an inexpensive journal.
- Offering a sister a compassionate hug.
- Sending a sister a positive affirmation text.

Locking Arms Together

Women are relational creatures who need and desire to express themselves through conversation and interaction. Fellowship and conversation for women is like water, sunshine, and fertilizer to a sprouting plant; without it, the plant will wither and die. Women within each of your circles need your spiritual, physical, and emotional impartation. A bearer of arms must be willing to lock herself to other women in order to offer them unconditional love.

Believe me, God has given you the wisdom you need to encourage and empower others to blossom and grow to maturity. Indeed, death and life are in your tongue. Therefore, by the Lord's admission, you must use the words of your mouth to feed and nurture them. Thus, give them the word of the Lord! If a sister needs love, give her love—unconditional, agape love. If she needs peace, offer her peace—unconditional, agape peace. If she needs patience, show her patience—unconditional, agape patience. Allow the nectar of your spiritual fruit to freely flow to others. In doing so, sisters everywhere can eat from the fruit of your tree and live.

When to Unlock Arms

> In fact, though by this time you ought to be teachers, you need someone to teach you the elementary truths of God's word all over again. You need milk, not solid food. Anyone who lives on milk, being still an infant, is not acquainted with the teaching about righteousness. But solid food is for the mature, who by constant use have trained themselves to distinguish good from evil.
>
> Hebrews 5:12-14 (NIV)

Up to this point, I've tried to encourage you to walk in love toward one another by offering your prayers, fellowship, and support. But tell me, what do you do if your acts of kindness become a yoke of bondage? When do you suppose it's fitting to unlock arms and walk away? When is enough enough? Although no one likes to accept or submit to defeat, you must know when it's time to unlock arms.

Many sisters disable other sisters by carrying them too long. Sisters who are not released after they are past the weaning stage will develop what I've labeled a "leeching" spirit. You'll find they are often needy and co-dependent, "just too big to still be in momma's house."When relationships become strenuous and there is no willingness to change, you must release yourself from the burden of responsibility. If you don't let them go, you are going to hinder their spiritual progress.

When you release sisters, it forces them to rely on the wisdom the Lord has provided. It also reminds you that you are not their source. God is! Regretfully, some sisters would rather be carried than stand on their own two feet. What these sisters really want is a handout—not support! No doubt, sisters with this mentality will leave your bosom only to find another willing enabler. Ideally, every sister you've spent quantity time lifting in prayer and intercession will in due season be spiritually, mentally, and emotionally, capable of lifting someone else. That's the whole purpose behind sister love.

Jesus told Peter, "I have prayed for you that your faith fail not; when you are strengthened go and strengthen your brothers" (Luke 22:32, KJV). In the book *The 21 Irrefutable Laws of Leadership,* John Maxwell shares this stirring childhood poem. It is a fitting close to such a meaningful chapter:

> There are two kinds of people on the earth today, Just two kinds of people, no more, I say.

> Not the good and the bad, for 'tis well understood That the good are half-bad and the bad are half-good.

> Not The two kinds of people on earth I mean Are the people who lift and the people who lean.

Ella Wheeler Wilcox (115)

Review Precepts

1. Building sister-love relationships are an essential part of life and ministry.

2. Overall, women need and want the fellowship of other sisters.

3. When you define and redefine those within your various circles, by default you can determine your level of sanity. *Selah.*

4. Preserving the wealth of an inner circle relationship is critical. Neither you nor your ministry will prevail without the loving support of those who hold up your arms. Always covet and value inner circle companions.

5. Reaching out to others, especially other women, means going beyond the comfort zone. Putting yourself in a position to minister to broken women is, for the moment, permitting yourself to walk in their shoes.

6. Regretfully, gossip and backbiting are a serious problem in our churches. Since fellowship and conversation is an intrinsic need for women, we must ardently scrutinize what we say and whom we say it to.

Passing the Torch

*I*n Dr. Phillip McGraw's book *Self Matters,* Dr. Phil, as he is famously known, says this about life: "Out of the thousands of thousands of people we've met, decisions we've made, and moments we've lived; in the context of significance, it all boils down to this: ten defining moments, seven critical choices, and five pivotal people" (90). Wow! How do you begin to comprehend that! If Dr. Phil's statement is true, how do you determine which moments, people, and choices have significantly changed the course of your life?

In the life of a believer, our world began the moment we made the decision to live for Jesus Christ. In that moment, everything changed! Our ten defining moments, seven critical choices, and five pivotal people were not the same moments, people, and choices prior to salvation. Where we were once slaves to our own selfish ambitions, Christ now governs the course in which we live. Because of Jesus Christ, our total purpose for life has changed. Paul said in 2 Corinthians 5:17, "Therefore, if any one is in Christ, he is a new creation; the old has gone, the new has come!" (NIV). Suddenly, life has new meaning, and we have been "called out of darkness into His marvelous light" (1 Peter 2:9, NIV). Heretofore, it is indeed a joy and a wonder to behold. Beloved, this means, above many other things, that we are no longer our own. We have been bought with a price! Therefore, our passion should be none other than to establish the Lord's kingdom in the earth—Christ, working in us and through us to fulfill his good pleasure.

Passing the torch is recognizing the responsibility of preparing others for the succession of ministry, and ministry is living and demonstrating the word of God in total succession.

God's Word is an immutable, indestructible, document of eternal faith and legacy. In fact, it is invincible! It will never die! The Bible tells us, "Heaven and earth shall pass away, but my words will never pass away" (Matthew 24:35, NIV). The world today is in need of a Savior; as it is lost in a cesspool of decadence and depravity: drugs, homelessness, pornography, violence, crime, deception, corruption, teenage pregnancy, perversion—saints, you name it! These are but a few of the many enemies we face on a daily basis.

Nevertheless, by the word of God, the blood of Jesus Christ, and the power of succession, we can pass the torch of salvation, truth, and discipleship from one person to the other, one generation to the other, that to the end we may save a few.

At times I question whether the church has lost its passion and concern for the lost. We're so busy doing church stuff we've overlooked the importance of doing God's stuff. Saints, we must earnestly desire to see people come to know Jesus Christ as their Lord and personal Savior. It is at this crossroad in life when moments, choices, and people, change—forever. I'm here today because of women like Kathy Burrell and Prophetess Cynthia Steele whose lives, ministries, and conduct, inspired and encouraged me to want to know Jesus Christ on a personal level. It wasn't what they said to me that won me to Calvary's cross, but how they lived and demonstrated holiness before me.

There is an old, African proverb that reads, "It takes a village to raise a child." I know my life is a testimony to the sacrifices others have made for me—not so much as to value my accomplishments as a college graduate, a registered nurse, or a preacher, but because I've been taught how to live my life as an example of the believer. From my very existence, God was grooming me for the continuation of succession—the preaching and passing of the torch. In fact, God was using people, places, and predicaments in my life to plant seeds of righteousness and determination in me. Therefore, I define succession as "success that leads to perpetual legacy." Thus, success is not what one has acquired or gained; rather, it is what one has learned from the experience and passed on to the next generation.

Building a Legacy

Building people is every believer's responsibility. Unlike cloning, succession and mentorship are words I choose to define people building. Good leaders recognize the value of impartation, and they teach, train, and prepare others to successfully pass the torch.

Succession in and of itself is both inevitable and unavoidable. In fact, at some point in time, things as you now know them will eventually change. Nothing in this life remains the same. As a result of that fact, you mustn't become too comfortable with where you are and what you are doing. Ministry is transitional, moving, and ever changing. It is not stagnant or cemented—and it was never meant to be. Thus, ministry was designed for change. Therefore, you must learn how to change with it.

As a wise and competent leader, you should teach and prepare those within your various circles to carry the vision, pass the torch, and continue the legacy— even in your stead.

Corporations worldwide have always valued the principles of succession. Just look at the track record of companies such as Walmart, Coca Cola, and Nike. No doubt, these CEOs' support the philosophy of succession and their longevity are proof. By and large, ministry is no different. It too is equally important for the legacy of faith to continue to advance in this untold generation.

There are five specific reasons why succession in ministry is an essential key to overall success:

1. The dynamics of the ministry could suddenly change.
2. The ministry may be forced to redesign positions or personnel.

3. You may be promoted or demoted in or out of a position.

4. You may be lead of the Lord to move in another direction.

5. You may succumb to sickness and/or death.

Much like the mainstream corporations, ministries benefit from seers and visionaries who position the institution for continuation and advancement. In John C. Maxwell's book *The 21 Irrefutable Laws of Leadership*, legacy is the most essential aspect of succession. In fact, this is a leader's greatest contribution to his or her team. Legacy actually parallels inheritance as it resembles the gift "a good man leaves to his children's children" (Proverbs 13:22, KJV). Just the same, legacy enables and empowers others to continue the mission of the institution while consummating the vision and embracing the promise. Again, Maxwell contends:

> *Achievement* comes to someone when he is able to do great things for himself. *Success* comes when he empowers followers to do great things with him. *Significance* comes when he develops leaders to do great things for him. But a *legacy* is created only when a person puts his organization into the position to do great things without him. (221)

Are You Ready to Accept Change?

One day, I was visiting my sister's home when I found an interesting book on her dining room shelf, *Who Moved My Cheese?* by Spencer Johnson. Dr. Johnson unveils the irony of change through the story of four little characters: two little mice named Sniff and Scurry and two little men named Hem and Haw. Each of these characters wanted and needed cheese to live and survive. Yet, to get to the cheese, they had to be willing to confront and accept change. Consequently, their response to change would either lead them to their survival and succession or to their fatal demise.

Of course, a few of the characters in the story overcame their struggle for change and succeeded. Others, however, did not. At any rate, the moral of the story is this: change is inevitable. Therefore, you can either accept it and prevail or become a victim of it and languish.

Succession and legacy requires us to accept, adapt, and overcome change. Better still, when change is not allowed to hamper, obstruct, or prohibit your progress, the legacy is bound to continue.

Even though some leaders govern their ministry under the auspices of a monarchial system, good leaders always discourage the one-man-show theology. They clearly recognize the importance of body ministry and purposefully empower every player with the resources needed to lift others as they lift themselves. I once heard it said, "Give me a fish and you feed me for a day, but teach me to fish and you feed me for a lifetime." *Selah*.

In a most urgent and immediate way, you must ensure that every member of your circle understands the vision. That's the only way you are going to be able to secure succession. Therefore, "write the vision and make it plain, so that everyone that sees it can take it and run with it" (Habakkuk 2:2, NIV).

My husband obtained our vision and missionary statement while overseeing Faith Christian Fellowship Church in Fussi Shi, Japan. The slogan "cultivated to grow and empowered to go" was actually birthed out of that experience. When we left Japan and began to pastor in England, I asked him if he was going to change the vision and missionary statement. I assumed new people, new work—new vision. Surprisingly enough, he said something I thought was utterly amazing. "No," he said, "this vision was not for a specific place and time. It was given to me as the cornerstone of my ministry. Everywhere I go, I'll take it with me. The vision is in me, and it doesn't change."

Sowing and Reaping

Do you know what dead works are? In a nutshell, dead works are wasted energy. Finally I've come to realize just how much time I've spent sowing into the wrong people. In fact, in the early days of my ministry, I actually wasted hundreds upon thousands of minutes sowing and reaping (practically) nothing. Come to mention it, I probably reaped (if there is such a thing) less than dead works. However, that was in the past.

Today, I invest my time, energy, and available resources on people who have the desire and the determination to carry the vision. These people are "potential carriers."

Since my husband began to pastor some fifteen years ago, he has always had, by the grace of God, a successful ministry. I've watched him embrace people—all kinds of people—smiling, sharing, and caring. Though he gives everyone in the ministry unconditional love, he diligently sows such aspects as time and resources into his leadership. He'd often tell me, "If I sow into them, they will sow into others."

After I became his co-pastor, I realized exactly what he was talking about. Ministries reproduce as sheep beget sheep. Therefore, I had to learn how to sow into those who could sow into others. In other words, it was all about procreation and reproduction—that is the ultimate goal.

If you sow into good ground, your legacy is ensured, and the continuation of your seed will abide in God's eternal promise. Beloved, don't waste another second! Time is of the essence. Therefore, you must carefully evaluate the seriousness of the hour. I now labor smarter and not harder. "As long as it is day, you must do the work of him who sent you. Night is coming, when no one can work" (John 9: 4, NIV).

There is a reason I'm so adamant about seed time and harvest. I want to guarantee the harvest I have begun planting. In fact, I don't want to see or hear that a single kernel has perished and fallen by the wayside.

For many years, the young airmen my husband and I invited into our home to share Sunday dinner with us have earnestly become the seeds sown into the harvest of my legacy. I, for one, have spent many hours on the threshing floor, praying and interceding for their lives. At times, I've compared myself to Rizpah, postured in the desert, swatting at the fowl birds and wild beasts that were aiming to oppose, corrupt, and desecrate my seed. Yet, in the midst of it all, God put a few young people in my life to inspire me to stay on course—to purpose to pass the torch. Every seed I've planted I claim as my spiritual offspring. They represent the fruit of my labor: my blood, sweat, and tears. This is what legacy is all about. Praise God! I can honestly say I've been faithful over a few things.

Lady preacher, legacy requires work, dedication, and sacrifice. You can't have increase without it. I adjure you, hold fast in the faith. Moreover, to produce a harvest, you must surely plant a field. Perhaps not every seed you sow will grow up strong and stout, but by all means, plant it anyway. I'm no horticulturist, but I leave you with a few important techniques for sowing and reaping a harvest—perhaps some direct keys to overall succession: orchestration, cultivation, organization, pollination, planning, articulation, prioritization calculation, and determination.

Beloved, you mustn't rely on fate or circumstance as a means of cultivating your seed. On the contrary, you must strategically watch over the seeds you've planted—allow their roots to go deep into the earthen soil, the good soil of the word of God. Always remember, whatever you plant today will produce for you a harvest on tomorrow. Whether the seed is good or bad, right or wrong, your harvest is the cornerstone to the legacy you construct.

Review Precepts

1. Jesus gave his life as a ransom for many. In return, he employs us to "take up our cross (daily) and follow him" (Luke 9:23). The call to ministry requires that we deny ourselves and follow him, leading and disciplining others as fishers of men.

2. You must sacrifice (lay aside) your will so his will can be done in you. Ministry mustn't ever be about you. In fact, if the ministry becomes more about you than him, immediately stop, halt, and reevaluate your purpose.

3. Those who encircle you expect you to impart succession and legacy into them. They are there because they value your teaching, and they desire to glean from your wisdom and experience.

4. Mentorship is essentially the crescendo of ministry.

5. Throughout your ministry, you are going to be sowing and reaping. However, it is important for you to sow into good ground so the seeds you plant will yield a fruitful harvest.

The Ten Commandments of Ministry

1. You shall seek the Lord thy God exclusively; yea, continuously, giving no place to the devil (Proverbs 3:5-6; 1 Corinthians 10:12-13).

2. Thou shalt not mimic, compete, or compare thyself to anybody else. Be thyself (2 Corinthians 10:12).

3. You shall show thyself approved unto God, taking advantage of every opportunity to increase in learning (2 Timothy 2:15; Hosea 4:6).

4. Thou shalt not make thine own way. God will reserve a place for you in your season (Genesis 41:1; Samuel chapter 16; James 3:16).

5. Thou shalt not use the Lord's pulpit or thy position to promote thine own agenda; manipulation, domination, and control is insidiously witchcraft (2 Kings 5:21-27; 2 Samuel 15:2-10; Galatians 6:7; 1 Peter 4:10-11).

6. Thou shalt not attempt to steal God's glory. You are absolutely nothing without him, and he will not share his glory with another (Galatians 5:26; 6:3-5).

7. You shall walk circumspectively (attentive and alert) with balance, humility, and a repentant heart, conducting thyself appropriately before others (2 Chronicles 31:21; Colossians 1:10-

12; 2 Thessalonians 3-11-12; Eph. 5:15; 1 Peter 1:15-16).

8. Thou shalt not covet the Holy Spirit's job. These are God's people, if he doesn't change them, they will not be changed (Colossians 4:5).

9. You shall honor thy spiritual authorities that you mayest obtain the Lord's blessing and his servants' favor (Hebrews13:7-17).

10. You shall surrender thyself to rest and relaxation so that you mayest enjoy the fruits of thy labor, or thou shalt surely perish at the hands of thy mission (Genesis 2:2; Exodus 18:13-22).

References

B. A. Robinson by Ontario Consultants on Religious Tolerance; *w.religioustolerance.org/chr_dira.htm*: 27 April 2000 to (latest update) 01 December 2005.

Gary Chapman, *The Five Love Language,* Chicago, Illinois, Northfield Publishing, 2004. Holy Bible (King James Version); Grand Rapids, Michigan; The Zondervan Corporation. *I've fallen and I can't get up*; Wikipedia, the free encyclopedia; *http://en.wikipedia.org/wiki/I've_fallen_and_I_can't_get_up*: 10 December 2005.

James Strong, *Strong's Exhaustive Concordance Of The Bible;* Thomas Nelson Publisher, Nashville, Tennessee, 1990.

Jerry Adler, Newsweek Magazine: Spirituality in America, *Special Report, In Search of the Spiritual* (Pages 46-63); 05 September 20005.

John Bevere, *The Bait of Satan;* Orlando, Florida, Creation House; 1994.

John C. Maxwell, *21 Irrefutable Laws of Leadership;* Nashville, Tennessee, Thomas Nelson Inc. 1998.

John Gray, *Mars and Venus Together Forever;* New York, New York, Harper Perennial, 1996.

Merriam Webster, *Merriam Webster' Colligate Dictionary Tenth Edition;* (Springfield Massachusetts: Merriam-Webster Inc., 1993).

Phillip C. McGraw, *Self Matters;* New York, New York, Simon & Schuster, 2001.

Samuele Bacchiocchi Ph.D., Professor of Theology, Andrews University. *Roles Within Marriage, Endtime Newsletter # 44; http:// w.greatcontroversy. org*

Spencer Johnson, *Who Moved My Cheese?* New York, G. P. Putnam & Sons, 1998.

Sue and Larry Richards, *Every Woman In The Bible;* Nashville, Tennessee, Thomas Nelson Publishers, 1999.

W.E. Vine, Merrill F. Unger Williams White Jr., *Vine's Complete Expository Dictionary of Old & New Testament Words;* Nashsville, Atlanta, London, Vancouver, Thomas Nelson Publishers, 1996.

Wikipedia the Free Encyclopedia. http://en.wikipedia. org/wiki/Greek_words_for_love

Youth Noise; *http:// w.youthnoise.com:* Share Your Problems, Noise Boards, October-November 2005.

Endnotes

Chapter 1. "Men and Women Together in Ministry" and "Are Women Supposed to Preach?"

1. Adam in the Hebrew means man, mankind, or human being: See page 2 of *Every Woman In The Bible*.

2. Sue and Larry Richards in their book, *Every Woman In The Bible*, describes in chapter one, *Woman in Creation and the Fall*, the consequences of women before and after the fall. The word *ezer*, Hebrew for (helper) page (4) and *ish*, Hebrew for husband or man page (8).

3. Once again Sue and Larry Richards make some very interesting points as they expound on the issues of 1) head coverings; 2) women speaking in the local assembly; and 3) mutual submission. The scripture references come from 1 Corinthians 11:5-12 and 14:33-34 and Chapter 14 in their book.

4. *Parakletos* is the Hebrew word for comforter; it is used to describe the Holy Spirit. The complete

interpretation is found in the *Vine's Complete Expository Concordance*, pages 110-111 (3875).

5. B.A. Robinson's general statistic's suggests that 50 percent of American marriages end in divorce. Christian Marriages were reported as higher than any other faith group.

6. Life Application Bible NIV, pages 2078-2079, commentates on Paul's reasoning for silencing the women in the churches; and also head coverings.

Chapter 3. *Alone With God*

1. Koinonia in the Greek means feelings, to feel or come to know through fellowship, communication, and exchange. See the *Vine's Complete Expository Concordance*, page 233 (2841). Also in the Vine's is the word Ginosko. Ginosko is a Greek word meaning "to know or perceive," to feel or to touch, page 232 (1097).

Chapter 4. *Waiting is Gain*

1. Back in the old church, the first few pews were referred to as the mourner's bench. It was so named because the mothers of the church or perhaps even the deacons would sit on those pews and summons God through songs and prayer. If someone needed deliverance, they sat them on the mourner's bench and instructed them in wailing and weeping. The mourner's bench was an anointed spot; many of God's

people were freed from demonic vices as they prayed there.

Chapter 7. *The Other Side of Ministry*

1. The story of Samson is located on p. 367 in the commentary notes of *The Life Application Bible* NIV.

Chapter 8. *Welcome to "Holywood"*

1. In the *Life Application Bible* NIV, page 1535, the commentator suggests for temptation to be "effective" it must be based on a real need.

Chapter 9. *Blind Leaders*

1. Dunamis is the Greek word for power, might, ability, and strength. This word is often used to describe the workings of the Holy Spirit. See the *Vine's Complete Expository Concordance*, page 478-479 (1411).

2. It would be in the greatest interest of a ministry if pastors, ministers, and leaders had some basic courses in psychology and human relations. I recognize such teachings are humanistic and secular in nature, but the information could, at times, be invaluable.

3. In Jerry Adler's Newsweek article, he share's some interesting statistical facts concerning religion in America today.

Chapter 10. *Fallen Angels*

1. The *vine's Concordance* references *sift* with the word *winnow*. Winnowing refers to the chaff which is blown away during the harvesting of wheat pg. 574. The commentary notes of the *Life Application Bible,* pg. (1723); denotes Satan's desire to "crush Peter and the other disciples as grains of wheat."

Chapter 11. *Healing for the Spirit, Soul, & Body*

1. The word Zoe comes from the Greek word meaning life. "Life as a principle," life in the absolute sense, life as God has it, that which the Father has Himself. In the English language zoo or zoology comes from the word Zoe. Pg. 367 (2222) in the *Vines Complete Expository Concordance.*

Chapter 12. *Sister Love*

1. The Vine's concordance gives many scriptural references to the differentiation of these first two definitions of love, agape (25-26) and philia or phileo (859) pg. 381-382.

2. Webster defines *eros* as a derivative of the word erotic which means relating to or dealing with sexual or physical love.

3. The Wikipedia Free Encyclopedia identifies a fourth kind of love, storge, known in the Greek as love expressed via natural affection; like that of a parent to a child or a child to a sibling or relative.